How to Turn Property Investing from a Job into a Business

Author: John A Foster Title: How to Turn Property Investing from a Job into a Business – The Trilith Way

ISBN: 978-1999-620103

Category: SELF-HELP/Property/General Publisher: Breakfree Forever Publishing

THE TRILITH WAY

JOHN A FOSTER

Dedication

This book is dedicated to the memory of my father, Trevor Foster, who was a great father and a great guy on all fronts. He taught me to be patient amongst other things and that you are never too old to learn, as he proved time and time again. To my mother, Adela Foster, who taught me Spanish and how to knuckle down and keep going no matter what. Both my parents always stood by me and told anyone that would listen how proud they were of me. To my sons, and extended family who I am proud of, and our grandchildren, for the fun and curiosity that they generate. To Georgina, who is my partner, both in life and in business, and who got me involved with property by persuading me to join a three-day basic property training course.

To my close friends, who I know I can call upon when needed – you know who you are. To the many friends I have made throughout my property and business journey who are dedicated and always ready to offer advice and have mentored me when needed.

To all of you, I would simply like to say Thank You.

Foreword

Whether you start a business in an effort to solve a problem, to offer a unique product or service, or to make money, you will need a profit to become sustainable. In the property business in particular, the aim for most investors is, first and foremost, to make a profit in order to build financial security for themselves and their families. I personally have been investing in property for over ten years; and I became financially free at the age of twenty-five. I met the author of this book at a training seminar in London and learned about his role as a quality improvement expert. As I knew how important quality systems are to business from my days of studying entrepreneurship at the Cambridge Judge Business School, I engaged in a conversation. This was my chance to see how I could improve my businesses going forward, and John was very happy to share his experiences. It was the start of a great friendship as well, and it is my pleasure to share a few thoughts on *The Trilith*, both as a property investor and as John's friend.

Let me start off with a few quick words on the author. John's career spans over 42 years and his main advantage over this period of time has been his experience in different sectors, and his ability to transfer processes that are common practise in one sector, to another sector where they had not been introduced before. John for example had picked up on methods that are employed in the manufacturing sector to implement systems and reduce waste and understood right away that these would be particularly interesting and relevant to property. John's advice in terms of using one of such quality principles of continuous improvement saved a company £750k in one instance. In another company John analysed a department and found that their processes to 'get things right the first time' was very rather poor so John added systems and then worked with the management team. The department went from medium performance to high performance, saving the company time and money by 'getting it right the first time' more often. The key in this case, is giving decisions, processes and systems enough thought before taking action.

Unfortunately, property investors that are just starting out often do not take time to think before acting. Too many times, people rush to get into the market as they are afraid that they will miss out on an investment opportunity. Instead of spending time to carefully study the market, build a strategy, consider the supply and demand, and implement a dynamic business plan, they unwillingly create unnecessary risks. These risks soon add up, and the amateur property investor consistently creates new and unnecessary tasks that have a detrimental impact on both the time commitment of the investor and the investment itself. As a result, people become trapped by their investment, which, on the contrary, was purchased to provide more flexibility and financial freedom.

Short-term thinking is one of the main reasons investors find themselves in this situation. We often consider 'saving time' as a positive business practice, but more often than not, because of this, corners are cut, and major long-term benefits are lost. With all of the uncertainty around the Private Rental Sector in the modern age, we need to build our property businesses with security and sustainability whilst thinking about the long-term approach. This, I am happy to say, is where *The Trilith* can help you.

Right First Time Property Investing, The Trilith Way tells the story of Nick and his wife Amanda. It describes how, initially, they intended to build up a large portfolio of properties in order to provide security for their family, but instead ended up caught in an investment trap. It was not until they met an old friend who provided them with the concept of 'quality and continuous improvement systems' that they were able to free themselves of the investment bind they were in and enjoy their returns of investment as they had intended in the first place.

This book will help you on your own journey to financial freedom by showing how vital it is to implement the systems of quality and improvement in your business from the very start. The quality models, procedures and techniques as explained in this book can be applied to all types of business as well as different property scenarios such as finding your investment area, building a team, organising the administration and paperwork, ordering stock, finding and managing tenants, refurbs and renovations. The impacts these systems can have are often underestimated, but I can tell from experience that addressing the issues covered in *Right First Time Property Investing, The Trilith Way* will make *the* difference.

Although I did not have this book at my disposal when I realised I could improve my own property and consultancy business Windsor Properties, I did have conversations with John which made me realise the amount of waste I had in my own business. By following the steps that he now wrote down in this book, I was able to tighten up my business practices, cut waste and implement quality systems. This enabled me to make progress faster and expand my business at a much quicker rate.

Having understood the importance of these improvements, I put a strong focus on quality systems when I mentor other entrepreneurs on their journey to develop their own prosperous business or property portfolio. This book in fact is an excellent starting point, and I encourage my mentees to consider it as part of their 'recommended literature'.

I further implemented much of the systems explained in this book in businesses that I co-founded more recently. The architectural firm Windsor & Patania, the pet-care company Cooper & Gracie, and the e-commerce training business Zest Training all benefited from such systems, exemplifying the versatility of the information in this book, and the diversity of sectors it can be applied to.

I invite you to take note of the lessons in the following pages, whether you are starting out or even if you have been in business or property investment for a long time. Quality and continuous improvement methods will give you a competitive advantage and transform your activities into a business that is stable, structured, systemised, sustainable and scalable. I wish you the best of luck with your endeavours and encourage you to strive for your own financial freedom.

Ryan Windsor

Director, Windsor Properties

And Windsor & Patania Architects

www.windsorproperties.com

www.windsorpatania.com

Introduction

'It is not the strongest of species that survive, nor the most intelligent. It is the one most adaptable to change.

- Charles Robert Darwin

This book came about because I wanted to apply my knowledge of quality systems, tools and techniques and continuous improvement to my property business, so I jotted down some notes and then, for my own amusement, started turning them into a story. I was discussing business and books with Ryan Windsor, a well-known and young entrepreneur and property investor, and during our conversation, I mentioned that I was writing this book for myself. Ryan was intrigued and asked me if he could read what I had written so far. I then sent him a copy of my draft. After a couple of days, Ryan called me and suggested that I complete the book and publish it as it had useful information that needed to be shared as it could help business owners and investors. From then on, Ryan pushed me until I completed the book.

Why the title *Right First Time Property Investing, The Trilith Way?* In order to have a great business you must get things right first time, otherwise you will be forever dealing with issues that can frustrate you or lead to stress. A trilith is a structure that consists of two vertical uprights and a horizontal piece that crosses over the top to form what can be described as portal. The most famous series of triliths is Stonehenge. This structure has survived for thousands of years which is a testament to its quality, the people who made it have left behind a legacy that has endured and they built it with rudimentary tools which shows their strength of character, so I would like you the reader to step through this portal and see how you can build a business that will endure the test of time. Most businesses start off with good intentions but as it grows, people can become overwhelmed. This is because they begin working in their business instead of on their business because they do not have systems, tools and techniques that can help them. This results in the business becoming neglected as it becomes a job that is too much to handle. Using the tools mentioned in this book will allow people to start thinking of their businesses in a different way with the objective being to be able to run their businesses as a business and not as a job, which will in turn lead to sustainable income. Landlords lose tenants and money because they have not been taught to use the power of quality and continuous improvement to maximise profits whilst still providing tenants with a home rather than a house. Maximising profit does not mean cutting down on costs of your products and services or corners. It means looking at your business as a system from start to finish and removing waste that does not add value to the system. This book will show you how to use Quality Tools and Techniques and Continuous Improvement through re-telling a business fable. Why a business fable? A majority of you will not want to enrol in a formal class for a few years to study what is perceived as a dry subject in quality and continuous improvement just to see if it will benefit your business. Therefore, I have included the basics in this book and to make it easier to read and absorb the information, I decided to turn this information into a business fable. Should you decide that you want to know more about the subject, I have provided a list of books and useful websites in the appendix section of this book, or you can contact me, and I will try to answer your questions.

To get the best out of this book, you must turn the information that is provided in these pages into action, because if you don't action things, this book along with your business will just gather dust rather than momentum. Landlords have a bad reputation because of the few rogues that make a bad name for the rest of us. There are great, good and mediocre landlords as well as bad ones; hopefully, the lessons in this book will help you become great landlords that provide products and/or services that will place you in a position of demand and earn you the respect for all the hard work you put in. Similarly, I hope the book will show you ways in which you can maximise your business to obtain good profits and get rewarded for your time.

If you feel that you have been inspired by this book to take action in your own property investment business, then I ask you to please help inspire other people within your network and new investors to do the same and show them how it has helped you, so that together, we can create great housing stock and world class landlords.

All characters and events in this book are entirely fictitious and if they resemble any people or events, it is purely coincidental. The only parts in this book that are not fictitious are the names of places, books that are mentioned, Quality and Continuous Improvement Gurus, Quality tools and techniques, the Continuous Improvement tools that are used to make improvements not only to property investment but also to any business from the manufacturing to service industry.

I am not a financial advisor. Any references to finance mentioned in this book are purely for narration purposes and not meant as advice. Should you need advice, please seek out an independent financial advisor.

John A Foster

Director, Trilith Group

John.foster@trilithproperty.com

Chapter One

"Due to the heavy fog, there is a delay in BA flight seven eight three flying to Birmingham for one and a half hours" announced the voice over the public-address system. "Damn!" thought Nick Carrington, "oh well, I may as well get a drink." Nick wandered over to one of the airport's cafés and stood in the queue waiting to be served. As he stood there, he looked around and over at one of the tables, he spotted the familiar face of a man that he had not seen since his days in college almost twenty years ago, where they both attended as apprentices from their respective companies. Nick ordered a cappuccino and approached the man at the table. "Hi Trevor, long time no see!". Trevor Maclean looked up from the book he was reading, his eyes focused on the man who stood before him, then smiled as he recognised Nick. He stood up, put out his hand and said, "Hi Nick, how are you doing?" Nick shook Trevor's hand. "I'm good thanks, can I join you?" "Please do." Nick drew up a chair and sat across from Trevor. "So, what are you doing up here in Edinburgh?" "I am working as a consultant on a local project. What about you?" Nick took a sip of his drink before answering, "I am looking at some property that I was thinking of buying." "Are you thinking of moving up here?" "No no, I am a property investor".

"Interesting," remarked Trevor. Nick and Trevor then began talking about old times and asking each other about the people they knew from their past.

Nick's mobile started ringing; he excused himself and took the call. Nick listened intently and began to frown as he spoke to the caller. "That is the third one in a row!, what is going on?" Nick listened to the reply. "Surely you must have some idea? Tell you what; I will come and see you tomorrow and we can discuss this." With that, Nick hung up and put his phone back into his pocket. "Problems?" Trevor asked. "Yes, I have another void in one of my properties and I don't understand why." Trevor sat back and gathered his thoughts for a moment before speaking. "Let me guess, your properties are being managed by agents you personally picked due to their proximity to your properties and how much they charged." Nick shook his head in amazement. "Actually, you are right, how did you know?" "It is what most business people do, even though it's the wrong thing to do." "What's wrong with doing that?" asked Nick. "You lose money." Nick was now intrigued. "What other way is there?" "Rather than giving you a direct answer, here is something for you to think about. Anyone can become a lettings or estate agent, you do not need any qualifications, and they are not vetted unless they belong to an association, yet the perception is that, they are experts all because they have a shop front and/or a website." Nick sat back in his chair and thought about Trevor's words. Trevor watched Nick as he sipped his drink and kept quiet as he could see that he was lost in deep thought. It was a good five minutes before Nick spoke. "I never thought about how qualified agents are to manage my properties before now, but you are right. But I really don't have time to manage my properties, so I don't know any other way to manage them." "You don't have to manage your own properties, you just have to learn how to select and manage your agent." "How do I go about doing that?" asked Nick. "You can start by sending out a desktop audit to all of the agents in your area, just to see the sort of responses you get. From there, you can start to whittle it down to a few likely candidates for your business." "What is a desktop audit?" Trevor smiled. "It's a fancy name for a questionnaire." Nick was starting to see Trevor in a new light "What did you say you do?" asked Nick. "I am a quality consultant who is currently doing a project for the Dalton Towers Group." Nick was impressed. Dalton Towers Group are one of the world's biggest property developers, who deal with everything from residential homes to huge multi-storied commercial properties for major players in the world of finance and business. "So, what are you doing for them?" Trevor took a moment to gather his thoughts, as he did not want to come across as arrogant or dismissive, as Nick had shown real interest. "Well, I am teaching them the sort of things that I have just discussed with you and for the same reasons. They wanted to streamline their business and were thinking of cutting jobs as this is the traditional way of solving things. However, their CEO, Lawrence DeMille, convinced the board to bring me in to re-evaluate their processes and systems. I am therefore looking into introducing Quality Assurance and Continuous Improvement." "I know it is a bit of a cheek, but could you teach me?" Nick asked attentively. Trevor took a minute before answering, "If I do, I will not be able to visit your operation often, so you will have to do most of the work. I can give you some contacts via media such as Skype." Nick breathed out a sigh of relief; he had unconsciously been holding his breath. "Ok, I am willing to accept that." Trevor focused and stared at Nick before replying. "There are some conditions. First of all, you will have to do things exactly as I tell you, and there will be things that you may feel uncomfortable with. I need you to involve your team at all levels. Even though you will be leading them, they have to be on board with all the changes." Nick nodded enthusiastically. "I can do that, and I'm sure that I can get my team to help. Now, for the sixty-four-million-dollar question, how much will you charge me?" Trevor smiled. "You can get me a residential property in Spain, you can decide what type and how big based on the results, and I just want it on the coast." Nick did some quick calculations in his head and decided that if he could make some major savings by then, it was a good deal. After all, if it was good enough for Dalton Towers, then he should take advantage of having the same person work for him, so he stuck out his hand and shook on the deal. "I will draw up a contract and send it over to you. Give me your contact details," Nick said as he pulled out his phone from his pocket. Trevor smiled at Nick's enthusiasm and then gave him his contact details and business card. Nick also gave Trevor his business card and was about to ask more details about the desktop audit when the announcement came over the public-address system for them to board their plane. Nick and Trevor found that they were on the same flight. However, they could not resume their discussion as they were on different seats and could not change them.

When they landed in Birmingham, Nick briefly talked to Trevor and informed him that he would first arrange a face-to-face meeting to start the ball rolling. They said their goodbyes, and each made their own way home.

Several weeks passed before Trevor rang Nick to arrange a meeting. "Hi Trevor, I thought that you had forgotten about me." "No Nick, I have just been busy, I did warn you it was going to be like this. I have next Tuesday free, so I am happy to spend the day with you if you're available." Nick quickly checked his diary. He did have a few meetings penned in, so he checked what they were about and decided that he could move them to another day. "That would be great Trevor; I am free from about eight if that's ok with you." "That's fine by me; I will see you on Tuesday, bye". That was a bit short, thought Nick. However, the guy is busy.

Trevor arrived exactly at eight. Nick let him in and made drinks for them. He then directed Trevor to his office so that they could begin their meeting. "How many voids have you had this year?" Nick pulled up a spreadsheet on his laptop and checked the figures. After a few moments, he replied, "I have had a total of seventeen". "What was the cost of those seventeen voids?" Nick consulted his spreadsheet again and added up the figures. "Ten thousand and seventy-five pounds." "Are you sure that that is the total cost?" Nick checked the figures again in case he had missed some, whilst Trevor looked on amused." Ten thousand and seventy-five pounds is correct". "Actually, it isn't. It has cost you a lot more than that." Nick looked puzzled. "How have you arrived at that conclusion?" "Let's breakdown those voids. How much have you paid to advertise those voids?" "I don't, it comes from the management fees." "So, do you pay less management fees for when the houses are occupied?" "No, it's the same fee." "Don't you think that you should be negotiating for a lower fee so that you pay less during occupancy and full fee when the place is empty?" "I have never thought about it; I just accepted their fees." "Did you go in and do some repairs, decorating etc. when you had the voids?" "Yes, but that's normal" "So you haven't included that in your costs?" "No, it is just taken out of a slush fund that is used for this sort of thing." "Who carried out the work?" "It was my handyman, he carries out all of the minor work; if there is anything major, then I get a builder on it." "So, do you pay your handyman for every job?" "No, he is on a set wage, so he gets paid regardless." "Ok, I want you to put his hourly rate against each of these voids, and how long it took him to carry out the refurb. Then I want you to cost the materials that were used on each property." "It is going to take me a while to put that together," replied Nick. "That's ok; there is no need to do it now. How much have you paid in council tax whilst these properties have been empty?" "I'm not sure" "Next, how much have you lost in savings interest by not having money from these voids?" Nick was furiously writing down the questions whilst trying to answer the questions. "I have no idea, as I have not taken this into account.""Ok, whilst empty, did you have the gas check done so they are recertified?" "Yes, I did, I paid for those separately." "What about insurance?" "I will have to check," he replied. Nick looked down at his list and was flabbergasted that he could not answer some of the questions, as he never gave them a thought. Trevor could see from Nick's body language that he seemed overwhelmed. "I am not expecting you to do it right away; however, I want you to know your numbers by our next call." "I will get it done; I just wasn't expecting to be asked so many questions as voids seem like a straight forward matter." "In Quality, we call it 'The Cost Of Poor Quality', also known as 'COPQ'." Trevor took out a pad and pens and proceeded to draw. "Think of it like an iceberg you only see what is above the water, which in this case is the voids. Below the water and out of sight, there is the greater and more dangerous mass of ice, which is all the questions that we have gone through." Nick liked the analogy of the iceberg as he could visualise it and see that Trevor was right; there was more to the voids than he first thought.

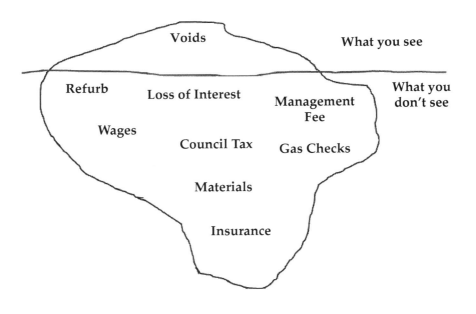

"I can see why Dalton Towers decided to hire you as a consultant; you have just blown me out of the water with what you have just shown me." "Thank you, but like this diagram, this is just the tip of the iceberg, there is still a long way to go." "I didn't realise that quality went into things like this." "There is a lot more to quality than people think, but it is based on some core principles." Nick was now intrigued "What sort of principles?" "We focus on our customers, because without them, we have no business and therefore no wages. Leadership is also important, as you need to understand your business and get people to buy into the organisation's vision. Involving people in your business is fundamental, as they are the ones carrying out most of the work. We look at your processes to ensure that they are working correctly, and then at your systems so that everyone knows how to do their job. Continuous improvement is essential as we can save money and time. We look at the facts through analysing data and carrying out a root cause analysis, and finally, we work with our suppliers to build relationships with mutual benefits." "Wow, I didn't realise that you look at all parts of the business, I always thought it was an inspection thing." Trevor smiled. "That is what most people think as this is the perception that has been formed in factories, but it is so much more than that." "I have heard of things called Lean and Six Sigma, which are something to do with improvements, but not as part of quality." Trevor sighed. "The West have split them away from quality and have created separate departments to use methods such as Lean, Six Sigma, Theory of Constraints, whereas in the East it is just regarded as quality. Let me show you what I mean." Trevor took out his pen and started drawing.

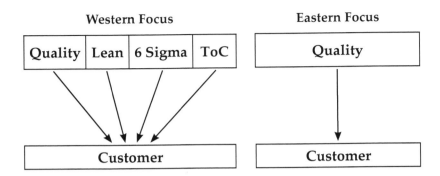

"So, as you can see, the West now have several methods of delivering good quality but the different functions don't communicate so things can get convoluted and political, whereas in the East, it is all about delivering good quality to the customer, so everyone is involved." "No wonder the East has a significant hold in the market place."

After a morning of going through spreadsheets and sorting through the issues, they broke for lunch. After lunch, Trevor suggested that they visit one of Nick's void properties so that he could see what was on offer. They got into Nick's Audi TT and set out on a twenty-five-minute drive that would take them to the Borough of Nuneaton. Nick powered his car through the B roads that took him through the small town of Meriden at the centre of England; he just loved these roads as he felt like he was on a Rally, especially with the power and grip that his car had. Trevor took in the views of the Warwickshire countryside as they sped through the countryside. Before long, they were pulling up outside a house that was at the end of a terrace on a small street. They stepped out of the car and Nick headed to the front door of the property as Trevor took in the street, the type of properties and their appearance. Nick took out a bunch of keys, opened the front door, and stepped in as Trevor followed. They moved through the small hallway and into the lounge where Nick turned the light on so that they could have a better view. The room looked a bit tired; the white walls were looking a little grey and the brown carpet was worn in places and parts of the skirting board that were scuffed and split. Trevor went over and looked at the windows and found that they were single glazed and that the frames were in poor condition. "As you can see, it's not too bad; a bit of paint and it will be ready to let again." "How many times has this house become void?" Trevor asked. Nick thought for a second and replied. "This is the third time." "Over what period of time?" "Over three and a half years." "So, on average, once a year? That is costing you money." "Yes, I can see that now, I guess I just need good tenants." "I think that you need more than just tenants, you need a new mind-set". "What do you mean?" asked a puzzled Nick. "Nick, this house needs more than just a lick of paint; you need to spend money on this property." "It's not that bad, and besides, I have a business to run and as you said, I need to save money," said Nick defensively. "Nick, you are missing the point, you save money by improving quality and taking wastes out of your systems and processes." Nick was not convinced and was beginning to have doubts about working with Trevor and wondering how much it would cost to get out of his contract. Trevor pulled out a notebook and a six-inch steel rule and began to draw; once he had finished drawing, he showed Nick what he had drawn and began to explain it.

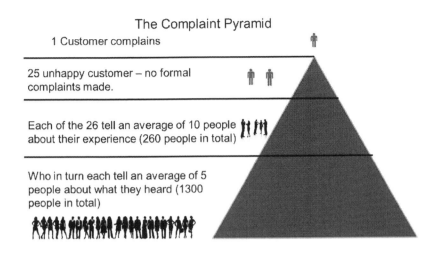

The Complaint Pyramid

1 Customer complains

25 unhappy customer – no formal complaints made.

Each of the 26 tell an average of 10 people about their experience (260 people in total)

Who in turn each tell an average of 5 people about what they heard (1300 people in total)

"In nineteen ninety-nine, TARP Worldwide produced this piece of research called the complaint pyramid, and you can see what the effect is from just three unhappy customers, which is what you have here. Now, fast forward to the present and the three complaints will reach far more people because now, there is social media so it becomes global; therefore your brand and business is going to take a huge hit, as people that you may want to do business with will be checking social media as part of their due diligence, and if they see lots of complaints, it gives them an excuse not to deal with you." Nick was shaken to the core as he realised there was a lot of truth in what Trevor was saying. "What do you suggest I do?" "If you agree, let me show you what can be done by using this house as your case study." "What will it cost?" "Let's take a look around the rest of the house and then we can make an estimate." With that, they explored the rest of the house and made notes as they went along. They came back to the lounge, looked at the list, and did some rough calculations. "I think that this can be done for about three thousand pounds," said Nick. Trevor disagreed. "I think that you need to double that figure." Nick was surprised. "I can get materials at a cheap price," he protested. "You may be able to get cheap materials but are they of good quality?" Nick was struggling to accept this and was furiously trying to calculate whether he should take the risk and go with Trevor when words from his old mentor came to mind. 'If you are not prepared to take risks, then you should not be in business'. "Ok I will double it; you can have a six-thousand-pound budget." Trevor smiled. "Believe me Nick, you won't regret it. I have a contact who is a trained project manager. I will give him a call and he will work with your construction team to facilitate the refurbishment." Nick put out his hand. "You have a deal." Trevor shook the proffered hand and they both smiled. They stepped back outside, got into Nick's car, and drove back to Birmingham, again using the back roads rather than the motorway.

They arrived back at Nick's home where they talked more about the house and Trevor asked him how long he thought it would take to complete the refurbishment. Nick told him that he thought it would take about six weeks; Trevor smiled and told him that he could get it done within four weeks. Nick was no longer surprised that Trevor could utter such statements but he made a mental note that he was going to take time out and see how the refurbishment would progress. Trevor then made a phone call to his project manager, Brian Davies, and asked him if he could take on the refurbishment and train Nick's construction team. Brian agreed, and Trevor gave him Nick's address and contact details. Brian told him that he would be over sometime next week; he would however confirm the date with Nick beforehand. Soon, it was time for Trevor to leave. They said their goodbyes and Trevor promised that he would call to see how things were going and to teach Nick more about the techniques that would help him run his business.

"Now, where do you think that we can make improvements?" "As Trevor mentioned, the refurbishments should be better, which falls in the processes." "Yes, you are right. So, let's take a closer look at it. At the top level, we need to complete the work to a high-quality standard, then it needs to be completed on time and finally it needs to be completed on budget." Nick nodded in agreement, as he couldn't disagree with what Brian was saying. Brian continued with his scrutiny of the process. "To get a high-quality finish, we need skilled contractors working with great materials, so we cannot cut corners here. Therefore, we need to look at our budget and how we can get the best out of it." "How do we do that?" He was genuinely interested, as this was an area that he knew he had cut corners to reduce costs. "We work with our suppliers; it is one of the principles of quality. Which suppliers do you use?" Nick just shrugged his shoulders. "I guess I just look around and see who has the cheapest deals at the time and buy from them." "That is part of your problem, you need to work with suppliers so that they understand your requirements, they know what your budget is and can work with you to fulfil your needs." "That is all well and good, but I won't have the buying power and so I will not get reduced prices," Nick complained. "Think about it, how many properties do you own?" Nick checked his spreadsheet, looked up from his laptop and said, "ninety-five". "So, ninety-five properties with an average refurbishment cost of six thousand pounds each, gives you a spend of five hundred and seventy thousand pounds. Do you not think that suppliers would love to have a piece of that action? Especially as you are still growing your portfolio?" Nick had not thought about his business in this manner and he was both shocked that he had overlooked something so simple and excited that he had help moving forward. "So, what do you suggest we do about it?" Brian considered the question and pointed at the process box. "We should standardise things as much as we can, such as paint colour, kitchen units, bathrooms, tiles etc. We can then decide on the suppliers to use and we will only use them and nobody else." "Your right Brian, I can see that now, thank you." "It is a good start that you have accepted these ideas and are willing to run with them." Nick was now curious. "If you don't mind me asking, how did it come about that Trevor helped you?" Brian smiled for a moment at the memory and then started to tell Nick his story. "After completing university, I went to work for a top firm as a project engineer. After a short period, I decided that I knew more than everyone else there as I was a hotshot and everyone else were just old farts, so I quit and set out on my own. I got my first contract and I was very arrogant; I thought I was the man. Other contracts followed but soon, I was so swamped that I started to cut a few corners. At first, they were just minor things that did not make much difference, but then, I started to cut bigger corners and I lost a contract. Word got out as the contract was with a big player and work started to dry up and I started panicking. Luckily for me, my university lecturer heard about my woes and suggested that his friend Trevor come and see me. At first, I had my doubts. After all, what could a quality consultant tell me about managing projects. How wrong I was. Trevor took my business apart and showed me where I had made mistakes and how to turn it around. At first, it was hard to get clients to give me a second chance, but I persevered, and I was finally given a small project. I turned it around on time and under budget, and so I was given a slightly bigger project again. The quality of my work stood out and they were impressed both by my work and by my new attitude. More work started to come in. I began to grow my business, and hired the right people that understood what was required of them after I had trained them. I have now gotten to the stage where the business runs itself, so I am free to pick the jobs I want to do for myself." "What made you decide to help me?" "Simply because Trevor asked me." "Is that it? Is that the only reason?" "Trevor must have seen something in you for him to ask, and that was good enough for me." "What do you get out of it?" Nick persisted. "I use the opportunity to learn more from Trevor, which means I can implement some of the things into my own business, and of course, by getting to know you, I expand my own network." The explanation satisfied Nick's curiosity and thinking back to his college days, he noted that Trevor was always the one that offered help whenever it was required and never expected anything in return.

Brian and Nick went through the list of suppliers that Nick had used in the past. Some Brian immediately dismissed, as they were small retailers that did the occasional sales. Once they had a list of possible suppliers, they contacted them to verify that they had certifications such as ISO 9001 as this would show that they had a quality management system in place, which meant that they were checked regularly through audits. They also investigated the sort of deals they could offer. They soon whittled the list down to just a few names based on price, quality of the product and delivery time.

They also picked them based on perceived customer service as they would rather deal with companies that had helpful staff rather than those that did not have good telephone manners. Brian looked up from the list. "How would you like to get even further reductions on the price?" Nick was very interested. "How?" "Well, it has occurred to me that you must have a network of other property investors, so why don't you combine your spending?" Nick's eyes widened in surprise. "You're right, why hadn't I thought of that before?" he asked himself. "Two reasons come to mind. First, you were ignorant of your own business as we have just seen from the SIPOC and secondly, I guess it is because you don't want to give too much information away because you believe that they will become real competitors and muscle in on your area." Nick slowly nodded in agreement. "You're right, I may have to recalibrate my thinking." Brian laughed, "I said the same thing to Trevor when he was sorting my business out." Brian agreed with Nick that he should make calls to people within his network and propose the idea of combining their spend to the suppliers that they had identified. Brian made use of the time by going into Brian's conservatory and sitting comfortably. He went into a deep meditation to clear and calm his mind.

Nick finished his last call and was feeling very positive; he had received a good response from his network. He decided to prepare some lunch for Brian and himself before going off to find Nick in the conservatory. Brian was reading an electronic book when Nick appeared with ham salad baguettes and a mug of coffee for each of them. Nick explained how his calls went as they both ate their lunch. After lunch, they went back into Nick's office and continued to look at Nick's business. "Ok, now that we have sorted out your material suppliers, let's take a look at your trades. Do you have a builder, plasterer, tiler, plumber, electrician etc. that you use all of the time?" Nick looked a bit sheepish. "No, I tend to find trades that are the cheapest as I try to keep the costs low." "I bet that the jobs took longer than expected, and that you had a lot of reworking to do after you did your snagging list." "Mmm, yes, now that I think about it, you are right." "So now we will have to find a trades power team that can carry out good quality work. We can start by ringing your lettings agent and asking them who they use or if they know of good trades." Nick rang the agents and found that they mostly used a handyman rather than trades as anything major was usually taken care of by the landlords. "Now what?" Nick asked. "We are going out for a ride." Nick grabbed his keys and they got in his car and set out. "Where are we going?" "Just drive around until we see some building work going on, then we are going to go and talk to the builders." They drove around for twenty minutes after which they came across a terraced house that had a builder's van outside and a cement mixer working away on the front garden. They parked the car and walked up to the open front door of the house. "Hello!" shouted Brian. A man of about thirty wearing grubby jeans and a checked shirt appeared. "Yes mate?" "Do you know a good builder?" The man scratched his head and looked up. "No, I can't say that I do." "Thank you for your time." They turned around and went back to Nick's car. As soon as they got into the car, Brian chuckled. "Well, he doesn't rate himself as a good builder or else he would have asked about the job." Nick smiled "Well, I'm glad that

I didn't hire him then." They drove around for another ten minutes before they came across another builder working on a semi-detached house. They could see someone filling a wheelbarrow with cement from a mixer that was located on the drive. However, unlike at the first builder's, this mixer was placed on top of a tarpaulin sheet so that any splashes of cement did not contaminate the drive. Brian also noticed that, although it was a few years old, the builder's van was well maintained and clean. They approached the house. As they reached the front door, a man in his late fifties wearing overalls and high Vis vest appeared. "How can I help you gentlemen?" "Do you know a good builder?" "Tell me about the job." Brian and Nick glanced at each other and Nick proceeded to explain that he had a house that needed refurbishing. Brian asked if he could see the work that was being carried out on the house. The builder, who was called Dave, showed them around the house and explained what he was doing and the changes that he had made to the house including extending the kitchen and adding an en-suite to the bedroom. Brian was impressed with the quality of the work and he noticed that whilst they were looking around, the rest of Dave's crew carried on with their work and took no notice of them. "Do you have a business card, as I would like you to take a look at the house I want refurbished." Nick asked. Dave reached into the top pocket of his overalls and removed a thin chrome coloured box, which he then opened and took out a couple of business cards and gave them to Nick and Brian. They in turn gave Dave their own business cards. "I won't be able to start working on your house for at least another week, as I have to finish this one. However, I can come and take a look at it and see what needs doing the day after tomorrow if that suits you." "That would be perfect." Brian replied. They shook hands and Nick and Brian went back to the car and headed back to Nick's house.

"It looks like we have a key member of your trades team, and no doubt Dave will know other trades that he trusts to do a good job." Nick agreed and thought that it had been a productive day; a lot of things had been sorted out in such a short space of time. It wasn't long before they were back in Nick's office. "Right, I believe we can use the rest of the afternoon looking at your documents, as paperwork is key to running any business. We can start with your tenant agreement." Nick went over to his small filing cabinet and took out a couple of box folders, opened one of them and took out the tenant agreements. Brian looked over them and noticed that there were some differences between the agreements. He asked Nick about them. "I was experimenting with different agreements as I came across different ideas or adapted them from ones that I have received from people within my network." Brian asked which one was the most recent agreement being used. Nick looked through the different documents and thought that he had found the latest until he glanced at another document and was not sure which was the latest. Brian looked amused at Nick's confusion, "I guess that you have just learnt a valuable lesson." Nick looked up from reading through the agreements. "What do you mean?" "Well, you have just spent twenty minutes looking through the agreements trying to figure out which is the latest document and you are still not sure. We could cost the time that you have spent. Let's put your time at Seventy pounds an hour and we divide it by sixty as there is sixty minutes in an hour and then multiply that by the twenty minutes that you have spent, which will equal twenty-three pounds and thirty-three pence." Nick had never thought about costing his own time before and it was a revelation. Brian continued. "This waste can be eliminated by enforcing document control. We can start by giving each type of document a title, and a unique number so that we can identify it, then we can give it an issue number and date. We can then create a spreadsheet that contains information about the document and keep it updated. We can create a folder for each document in your computer that shows the latest document and within it, we can create an archive folder, so that when you make changes, you do not delete the document, you just archive it, so that we can trace the changes in case we decide that we need to check a previous version due to legalities etc." Brian's explanation suddenly made sense to Nick, so he invited Brian to show him what he meant. Brian created a folder, then created a number of documents, gave them a unique number and a title, and saved them to the folder. He started each document number with the letters TP. Nick asked him about this and Brian explained that he used the letters as the initials for The Properties, and that Nick could change it at a later date if he wanted to. A couple of hours later, Brian had finished. He showed Nick the result.

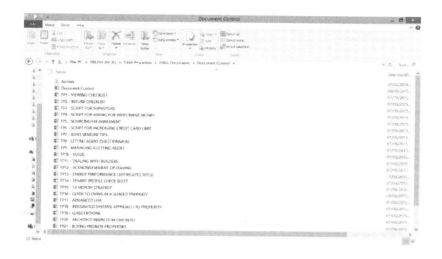

Brian then showed Nick the spreadsheet that he had created as an index and explained that he had hyperlinked each of the documents so all Nick had to do was click on it rather than searching for the document.

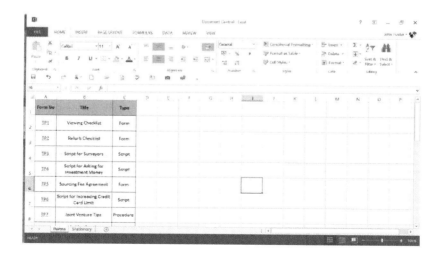

Nick tried it a few times and was impressed. "That's great! I would have never of thought of doing anything like this." "Well, if it's any consolation, I was no different, it was Trevor who showed me how to cost my time and how to apply document control to my business and it has made my life so much easier." It was late in the afternoon and they decided to call it a day and resume again in the morning. Nick suggested a breakfast meeting to start off their day and Brian agreed. Nick sat down and reflected on his day; he had learnt a lot about running an efficient business and a lot about himself. He thought that he was quite astute in business, but the reality was that he had been lucky to get this far without getting his fingers burnt, as he knew that he had cut corners to try and save money. However, from what he had learnt today, he could have cut costs by working smarter and being more efficient. He was looking forward to seeing what the morning would bring and what he would learn. The book that Trevor recommended came to mind and he retrieved it and began reading it in earnest. Nick's wife, Amanda, arrived at the house and did not think that Nick was home as the television was off and the house was so quiet. She was startled to see Nick in his office reading and amused by the look of concentration on his face. "How was your day?" Nick looked up. "Unbelievable!" Nick went on to explain what he had learnt and what they had done and showed Amanda the files and spreadsheet that Brian had created. Amanda was genuinely interested as she was the one that normally took the calls from the agents and usually managed them and was determined to see first-hand what Brian had to teach.

Chapter Three

Brian arrived early the next morning and was greeted by Amanda who introduced herself and then showed Brian through to the large dining room where Nick greeted him. Nick had set up two monitors that he had connected to his laptop so that they could all have a better view if required. Amanda went off to the kitchen leaving Nick and Brian chatting whilst she prepared breakfast. A short time later, Amanda appeared with a large plate of bacon sandwiches made with freshly baked bread and drinks. They settled down and Brian began, mainly for Amanda's benefit, with a summary of what they had learnt so far. "What is the most important part of your business?" asked Brian. Nick and Amanda considered the question. "I would say cash flow," replied Nick. "For me, it's having a portfolio that allows us to have financial freedom." Brian jotted down both answers on a pad that Nick had provided for each of them, and then looked up. "Actually, you are both wrong. The most important part of your business is your tenants, because without them, you would not have a business." Brian waited for his point to sink in and watched as Nick and Amanda looked at each other and nodded in agreement. "So how do you know that your tenants are satisfied?" Nick turned to Amanda as she answered the question. "The agents do the checks and if there are any problems, they inform us." Brian smiled "You are reliant on the agent who is also managing your property. Do you really think that they will actually tell you when there is a real problem?" "When you put it like that then I guess it is not in their interest to tell us." Amanda replied. "So, what do you suggest?" asked Nick. "We should create a form so that we can carry out a customer survey. We can then post it out to your tenants and they can either complete it and return it in a pre-paid envelop or they can download the form from your website and complete it and email it back. By doing this, you will have a better idea of what your tenants think about their experience." "That sounds like a great idea! What do you think Nick?" "I agree, let's do it." Brian began by asking Nick and Amanda what sort of questions they should ask. They had a brainstorming session; they soon had a long list of questions. Some of the questions were very similar so they decided to group them together and then they looked at each question on its merit and some they decided to disregard as not being relevant to what they were trying to find out. Once they had their set of questions, Brian began to construct the form. Nick and Amanda watched as the form came together and made suggestions to frame the questions a little better. The form was soon complete and they read over their handy work and were pleased with the outcome.

Tennant Survey

Please complete the following survey, as it will help us to make improvements to your experience whilst you are renting our property. When you have completed the form, either return it to us in a pre-paid envelop or email it to us at nacproperties@email.com

Agent's Name: _____

Questions	YES	NO
1. Have you reported any concerns to the agent in the last 12 months? (Give details)		
2. Was the agent helpful? (Give details)		
3. Is the agent quick to respond to your queries? (Give details)		
4. Was the work carried out in a timely manner? (Give details)		
5. What improvements could be made to the current property?		
6. What improvements could be made in regards to the agent?		

Note: If you need extra space to give your answer, please use the back of this form or a separate piece of paper.

Thank you for your help and cooperation.

Form TP 28   Issue 1   21/02/16

"I think that, although the form only has six simple questions, it captures what we need to know about the property and the agent." Nick and Brian agreed. Brian looked at his watch, "I forgot to mention, Trevor is going to skype us a little later; in the meantime, let's look at putting together a survey for the agents, as this will tell us more about them and how they operate." Nick and Amanda were enthusiastic and immediately began brainstorming questions with Brian. After about an hour and a half, they stopped to take a break and have a drink as they got ready for Trevor's call.

They sat around the monitors and Nick logged into Skype and waited for Trevor to come online. They did not have to wait long as Trevor was punctual. Trevor greeted them and asked how it was going. They explained what they had been doing over the last couple of days and took note of the progress they had made so far. "Ok that is a great start; however, I want us to go back to your documentation. You mentioned that there were different versions and I take it that that is still the case." Nick confirmed that Trevor's assumption was correct. "We need to sort that out and create a standard agreement document that we will use for all tenants, so you need to decide on what you require in your agreement. By standardising your documents, all your tenants will have the same document, and you and your agents will not be scratching your heads trying to figure out which agreement your tenant has. The consequences of not doing so include losing your case in court on a technicality, so we mitigate the risk by standardising everything." They agreed that they would review the documents as Trevor suggested. "Also, I suggest that you think of standardising all areas of the business from documentation to the actual refurbishments." "That's a big ask, as there is a lot to do and think about," replied Nick. "Yes, it is Nick, but if you don't do it, the cost in time and money will be even greater. Brian, can you please explain to Nick why you can be with him right now, instead of running your own business." Brian cleared his throat, "I was just like you Nick, and Trevor convinced me to standardise all my documents, processes etc. At first, I was reluctant as it seemed like it would take more time than I had but I went along with it. What I found out was that, because everything is standardised, I do not have to micromanage, which means that it has freed me up to be able to think about the bigger picture and it allows me to be away from the business; otherwise, all I will have created is a job for myself and not a business. If you think about it, the reason why the major fast food outlets are so successful is because they all do the same things in the same way no matter where in the world they are located, and that is one of the secrets of running a great business." Nick nodded reluctantly as he was taking it all in, whilst Amanda was enthusiastic. "Nick, this would make my life so much easier when dealing with agents, organising materials etc. and it would mean that we could employ someone that could run the admin side of the business." "Looks like I don't have a choice now," Nick chuckled good-humouredly whilst looking at Amanda's smiling face. "Nick, have you worked out the costs I asked you to do?" Trevor asked. Nick gave Trevor the figures and it was a lot more than he had expected; he was glad that Trevor had made him look into it. They made arrangements for the next call with Trevor, said their farewells, and ended the call. "I didn't see that coming." "I thought that Trevor may have waited a little before introducing standardisation, but I guess he is right, the sooner you start, the easier it will be, because once you get going on this journey, it will snowball and then you really won't have time," Brain replied. Amanda agreed with Brian as she could see the bigger picture and wanted to run with it.

"Before we start standardising everything, remember that we have our builder, Dave, coming over to look at the house, so we better think about what needs doing in the house. Have you got the floor plans Nick?" Before Nick could say anything, Amanda got up and went out of the room; she appeared a few minutes later with the plans of the house. She laid them on the table as they gathered around to view and discuss them. "I think that we need to not only carry out a refurbishment but also make upgrades to the property to make it more desirable." "What have you got in mind Brian?" asked Amanda. "Well, we could look into putting an extra bedroom, an en-suite, or a conservatory, anything really that could add value." They had a brainstorming session, discussed ideas, and sketched them out to see if the ideas could work. In the end, they decided that they could add an en-suite and a conservatory. It was late in the afternoon by the time they were finished and they decided to call it a day. They were pleased with what they had achieved and were looking forward to tomorrow when they could go over the house with the builder.

Brian arrived early at Nick's house and was greeted by Amanda who led him to the living room where he found Nick sipping a drink and reading a book. Brian smiled as he recognised the cover of the book. "So how are you finding Deming?" Nick looked up from his book. "It is a little bit technical for me in some places; however, I recognise some of the principles and a lot of the things that he says make sense." "You will find that once you have read it a few times, more and more will make sense. That's because you will have experienced some of the things that he talks about, so you can identify with them." "How many times have you read it?" "So far, three times, that's because I make it a habit to read it once a year." Amanda came in with a mug of coffee for Brian and they chatted about what had gone on over the last couple of days whilst they waited for Dave to show up. About an hour later, the doorbell rang, and Amanda excused herself to go and answer it. A moment later, she returned with Dave in tow. Brian and Nick shook hands with Dave as they greeted him. "Would you like a tea or a coffee?" Amanda asked. "No thank you, if you don't mind, can we go and see the house as I have a lot to do today." With that, they quickly organised themselves and decided it would make sense to go together in Amanda's car, so they all got into her Jaguar and set off to Nuneaton. They had a pleasant twenty-five-minute journey chatting away and getting to know each other a bit more before pulling up outside of the house. When they got out of the car, Dave looked up and stared at the roof. "You have a couple of broken tiles and the chimney needs pointing." The others looked up and after a few moments and with Dave's help, they saw the broken tiles and agreed with him about the pointing. They went inside and had a good look around. Dave was tapping walls and looking into all of the nooks and crannies and bouncing on the floorboards. He then went outside to look at the building and the garden, before heading back to meet the others. "What are your plans?" he asked. Nick responded, "we would like a refurb to a good standard, so new windows, bathroom and kitchen. Also plastering, painting and decorating. We were also thinking of putting in an en-suite and a conservatory. Ideally, we would have liked an extra bedroom, but we know that is not possible." Dave stroked his chin in deep thought as the rest watched him in anticipation. "I think that you will need more than that to bring this house to a high standard. Some of the floorboards are rotten and will need replacing. The wiring is dated and doesn't meet current regulations; your boiler is also inefficient, so it would cost a lot to heat the rooms. If you want another room, I can put one in for you." "We have looked at the plans and can't see how you can get another room in here." Nick responded. "A house is just a box, and you can do anything with a box and having looked at the attic, I can give you a loft conversion that will give you a double bedroom all en-suite plus built in storage." Nick's face beamed at the suggestion. "Now why didn't I think of that?" "Because, you're an investor not a builder." Dave quickly shot back. They had a good laugh and Nick got some good-humoured ribbing off Amanda. "So how much do you think this will all cost?" Brian asked. Nick and Amanda suddenly became serious as they waited for Dave to reply. "With the architect, loft conversion, the conservatory, two en-suites, bathroom, kitchen, boiler, rewiring plus the other works and landscaping, I would say that we are looking at between £30k and £40k." Nick whistled. "That is a bit more than I expected." Before Nick could say anymore, Brian chipped in, "what if we supply the materials?" Dave thought about it for a moment. "If you supply all of the materials, then I could do it between twenty and thirty thousand pounds." Amanda took hold of Nick's hand. "Will you excuse us for a minute?" With that, she took Nick outside so that they could talk in private. "Nick, I know that look, you were just about to say no, but before you do, I want you to reconsider." Nick interrupted, "Hun, it is a lot more that I am willing to pay. I can do a quick makeover for about three thousand pounds and quickly get a tenant in." "Nick, this house has already had several makeovers in the time that we have owned it, so you have probably spent more than Dave's estimate over the years and our tenants are not long term." "It's still a lot of money," he argued. "Tell me Nick, why did you ask Trevor for help?" "I guess it was because he made sense and he could help us save money. However,…" Amanda held up her hand. "Just stop right there Nick. You asked for help to save money. In the last couple of days, you have been given a taste of how we can do that, right? I think that redoing this house, so it can meet the high standards suggested is going to show us more." Nick was quiet as his mind was in turmoil, so Amanda decided to give him another push. "People pay good money to get an education so as to learn how to get ahead in life. Think of this house as our university fee, so that we can get ahead in our business." Nick stared at Amanda before answering, "I can't say that I am happy about it, but it's hard to disagree with you, and besides, we are doing a major refurbishment on this property." Amanda flung her arms around him and kissed him. Nick then realised that this meant more to Amanda than he thought. They strolled back in hand in hand. "When can we start?" Nick asked. Dave smiled. "Not just yet as we will need planning permission and that may take a while." Brian chipped in, "Dave, I take it that you know plumbers, electricians etc. that we will need to refurbish this house, right?" Dave nodded and told them that he only used trades he could trust to do a good job. Brian explained that he will project manage everything and he would like to meet the other trades as soon as they had permission sorted out. Dave had another quick look around the house before they left and returned to Nick's house.

When they arrived, Dave bid them farewell and climbed into his van and headed off to the current property he was working on. The others watched him go and then went into Nick's house; Nick and Brian went into the living room whilst Amanda went off to make them all a drink. Brian made a phone call to an old friend who was a town planner to set the wheels in motion for the planning permission. Amanda returned with cups of coffee and biscuits and they chatted about the house whilst they were having their break. "What's next?" Amanda asked. Brian thought about it for a moment. "As we already have a tenant questionnaire, I think we need to look at making a questionnaire that we can use to evaluate the lettings agents. After all, if you are going to use them to manage your properties, you need to ensure that you are getting value for your money." Nick and Amanda agreed that it was a good idea, so they began to brainstorm the questions that they would like to include. Brian was scribbling the answers down as they were being shouted out. After about an hour, they had run out of questions, so Brian began to group the similar questions together. They then went through the questions again and eliminated some as they were not really relevant. It wasn't long before they had a list that they were happy with and ready to put into a questionnaire format. Brian went to work using Nick's laptop and began to create the form that they would use. When he finished, they gathered around the monitor and checked over it, making some minor changes as they went along. Brian printed the questionnaire so that they could see what it looked like on paper. They each took it in turns and read it to make sure they were happy with the result. "Isn't this a desktop audit?" Nick asked. "Yes, that's exactly what it is." "Trevor mentioned it to me when we met in Edinburgh, now I understand why it is important." "We call it a questionnaire so as not to scare the agents. If we call it an audit, they may panic as it sounds more authoritative." Nick smiled, as he could understand how they would feel.

Letting Agent Questionnaire

We are property investors and we are considering buying properties in your area that we would like managed locally. In order for us to place you on our supplier list, we would require that you complete this questionnaire and return it to us with copies of any documents that we have asked for.

Please use a separate sheet of paper if you need to expand your answers

Question	Answer
1. How quickly after you receive the tenant's money will you put it into the landlord's account?	
2. How frequently will you pay visits to inspect the property?	
3. What do you look for when you do inspection visits? *(Provide a copy of your checklist if you have one)*	
4. If maintenance work is required, who do you call?	
5. Are your maintenance people members of the appropriate bodies, e.g. NICEIC for electricians, IPHE, etc., for plumbers, Gas Safe Registered for gas?	
6. Do you check maintenance people's membership for their appropriate trades?	
7. Will you arrange for the annual gas safety check?	

Question	Answer
8. Do you have a special telephone number for tenants to call for maintenance purposes out of normal office hours? *(Please provide the number)*	
9. How quickly will someone be on site if there is an emergency such as a burst pipe?	
10. Do you request an estimate of routine works first?	
11. Will you clear cost of work with the landlord or just go ahead?	
12. Above what money will you request authorisation from the landlord?	
13. Can you advise what the average cost of a sample of typical maintenance job is?	
14. What money float do you require to be provided to cover maintenance?	
15. How will you invoice the landlord for maintenance work?	

Question	Answer
16. How frequently will you send statements?	
17. Are you a member of a property ombudsmen scheme? (RICS, NAEA, NALS, ARLA or UKALA) *(please provide evidence)*	
18. How do you protect tenant's_deposit money?	
19. What are your procedures at the end of the tenancy, including hand-over of the deposit?	
20. If it is an HMO, do you have experience inof managing this kind of letting?	
21. If a landlord's licensing scheme applies locally, how do you deal with this?	
22. What percentage (%) is your rent arrears rate?	
23. How will you market the property?	
24. Is there a finder's fee?	

Question	Answer
25. How do you vet the tenant?	
26. What references do you ask for from the tenant?	

Form completed by:

Position: _____   Name: _____

Signature: _____   Date: _____

On completion, please send it to the following email address, using the subject line 'LA Questionnaire':

nacproperties@email.com

Thank you for your cooperation

They broke for lunch and Brian called his office to check in. He knew that if there were any problems, they would have called him, as majority of the time, they sorted things out themselves as his team was very competent. Nick checked his emails and Amanda booked her and Nick onto a local network meeting. After they had finished their lunch, Brian suggested that they do a little problem-solving exercise to understand why they were getting voids. Nick hinted that the problem was that the tenants always wanted more from the property whilst paying less for it, so they were always chasing the shiny penny and he had to find new tenants because of it. Amanda thought that there was more to it than that and that Nick was being too simplistic. Nick was about to disagree when Brian suggested that they make a start on the exercise so that they could get to the real root cause and know what the real problem was. He asked Nick if they had a whiteboard that they could use. Nick went out to his office and reappeared a moment later with a board and some marker pens. They laid the board flat on the table and gathered around it as Brain began to draw on it. He started with a single line and then drew a box at one end of the line.

"We need to come up with a problem statement." "That's easy, voids," replied Nick. "Sorry Nick, but that is just not good enough. Let me explain. If we do not have the right problem definition, we cannot get to the proper root cause. An example would be if your tenant told you that they had a leak. You would then have to investigate the whole property to find out where the leak was. However, if your tenant said that there is a leak coming from the bedroom ceiling, which is sodden and that began on Tuesday during the big storm and has been leaking on and off ever since, you would then know where the leak is. You would also have a rough idea of what damage it has done, when it started and that it has been an intermittent problem since then. From this, you would quickly guess that you may have a problem with the roof, so you would start your investigation there, which will in turn save you a lot of time and effort." "That makes a lot of sense. Don't you think so love?" Nick nodded. Brian tapped the box that he had drawn with his marker pen. "So, what's the problem definition?" "How about 'voids are on the increase'?" "That's good Amanda but I don't think we are there yet." "How about 'voids have increased over the last year'" "Very good Nick, but let's add more to it. How much of an increase have you had?" "Fifteen percent," Amanda volunteered. Brian wrote the problem statement in the box.

Voids have increased by 15% in the last year

"Now, we need to come up with headings for areas that may contribute to the problem." Brian now drew some more lines.

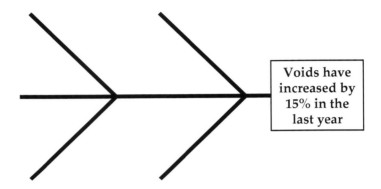

"That looks like a skeleton of a fish," observed Amanda. "Actually, this is known as a fish bone diagram. It is also known as a cause and affect diagram, but the proper name for it is an *Ishikawa diagram*, as it was created in Japan by Kaoru Ishikawa, who pioneered quality management processes in the Kawasaki shipyards. This was adopted by other manufacturers and eventually became one of the seven tools of quality. It is often combined with brainstorming as the suggestions are added to the skeleton under individual headings. It is a powerful tool as it is visual and if you keep adding on to it, you will eventually get to a saturation point, so you can be sure you have thought of every possibility and then, through elimination, the most likely causes will come to light, and they are the ones that we can investigate further. Some headings that I am going to suggest are environment, price, people and property." Brian drew them on the Ishikawa diagram as Nick and Amanda watched.

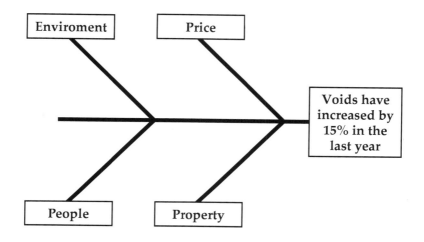

"Ok, now let's put bones on the fish, using these headings." Nick and Amanda started out slowly but soon got into the swing of it and Brian wrote down all of their suggestions until they had exhausted all avenues. They looked over the Ishikawa to see their handy work.

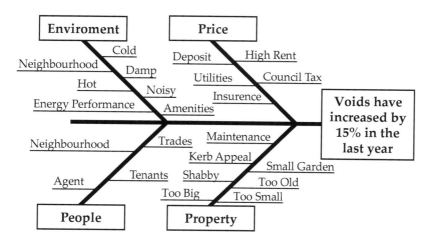

"By grouping them into categories, you can certainly see where the problems are. Can you have more categories?" Nick asked. "Depending on what you are trying to investigate, you can have as many as you would like, but it becomes a bit unwieldy, so try to keep it to four or six categories." "What do we do now?" Amanda asked. "We can now try to decide which are the most likely candidates contributing to your voids and do something about it, that is, if we can." They looked over the Ishikawa and talked about each sub-heading in each of the four categories. They eliminated some for the moment and some they discussed further until they came up with a list that they thought was causing the voids.

1. Shabby property

2. Wrong tenant

3. Energy performance was too low

4. Rent is too high

"Right, let's take a look at the first problem on the list. Why is the property shabby?" "I guess it's because I have spent as little as possible on it," replied Nick. "Why?" "To reduce costs." "Why?" "To maximise my profits of course." "Why?" "To create more wealth." "Why?" "To be financially free so that I can do what I please. Why are you asking?" Nick asked as he was getting flustered at Brian's questioning. "Bear with me Nick; this is a technique called the five whys. The theory behind it is that by the fifth why, we get to the root cause. In reality, you can get to root cause in as little as one why or as much as ten plus whys. So, why did you want to become financially free?" "Because, I was brought up on a council estate and I'm never going back there." Nick got up, excused himself and went out of the room. Amanda decided that she needed to give Brian an explanation. "You will have to excuse Nick, you have touched a nerve. You see, he hated living on a council estate as most of the kids at his school lived in their own homes and they treated Nick as if he was a poor kid, so essentially, he was verbally bullied. He did well at school, got himself an apprenticeship, and started saving some money. One of the guys that he worked with suggested that he should get into property and so Nick bought his first house and instead of renting it, decided to move out of his parent's home and into his new property. He went along to a property network meeting and they explained to him how he could build up his portfolio. After he had acquired a few houses, he suggested to his parents that they move out of their home and into one of his properties. His parents turned him down as they lived near all their friends and they were happy there. Nick just could not understand that, so he walked away and has not spoken to his parents in about thirty years. When we got married, he didn't invite his parents, despite me asking him to and I don't know where they live so I couldn't go and talk to them about it." Brian thought about how people can make things difficult for themselves because they didn't understand other people's point of view. Maybe this process will help Nick see things differently. Nick appeared with a tray of coffee mugs and began handing out mugs. "I thought it was time for a short break," he explained awkwardly. Amanda gave him a knowing look that Nick ignored as he sipped his drink. They had a general chit chat as they drank their coffee and the atmosphere in the room soon lightened as they relaxed. "Back to work," Amanda suggested after a suitable amount of time had passed. Brian took his marker pen and wrote the first root cause as financial freedom. "Now that we have a root cause, how are we going to fix this?" Nick and Amanda stared blankly at the whiteboard. "I'm not sure that we can," said Nick after a few thoughtful minutes. "We need to change your mind-set. As someone once said to me, don't look at the cost of the shovel when your digging for gold. This is what you are doing Nick, we can maximise your profit through other methods. You have made a start by talking to suppliers and people within your network so as to get reduced prices. Another way is to have a good quality spec home so that you are able to ask for and get a higher rent, which is what we are going to do with your Nuneaton property. You will also reduce your costs by standardising the way you do things. Can you see where we are coming from?" Nick nodded. It had started to make sense. "So, making more profit entails making little step improvements," Amanda stated. "You have hit the nail on the head. Remember back in the day when Japanese cars were little rust buckets sold with all the extras that you didn't have to pay for? Then over the years, they became more reliable and less prone to rust? Whilst the rest of the world kept on producing the same type of cars, the Japanese ate into the car market little by little until they become big players by producing great cars that were smooth, quiet, stylish and reliable. By the time the rest of the major car manufacturers caught on, the Japanese had become the major force in the industry. They managed to do this by continuously improving their processes so that they could make big inroads into the industry and get paid quicker for the goods that they produced. They began to teach the West what they were doing. We have therefore learnt from them and we are now applying their tools and methods in all sorts of industries. The ironic thing is that, they learnt a lot of the tools and techniques from quality gurus like Deming and Juran which they applied with gusto whilst these gurus were mainly ignored in their own country." "So, why did the Japanese teach us what they were doing, seeing as they had a competitive advantage?" Amanda asked. Brian was impressed with Amanda; she seemed to grasp things quicker than Nick. "Great question. Well, the Japanese are so far advanced that they knew that by the time the West caught up, they would be years ahead. So the West are still playing catch up. However, they also recognised that, by helping us in our industries, we would be helping them improve the supply base, so they could source things that were of good quality and at a cheaper price. History lesson over, let's get back to work. Why do you term your tenant as 'wrong'?" "They are not long term." "Why?" "They have been vetted wrongly." "Why?" "The agent hasn't done it correctly." "Why?" "I don't know," admitted Nick. "Have you informed the agent of the type of tenant you want in your property?" "No, we have relied on the agent to get the tenant based on their own experience," Amanda replied. Brian wrote down a second root cause was that there was no model of the type of tenant they wanted to pass on to the agent. "Remember, you are in business and you have to manage your agent. You can only do this when you have a clear understanding of what your requirements are." "Ok, let's go on to energy performance," Amanda said enthusiastically.

"Why is the energy performance low?" "Because they are old houses." "Why haven't you modernised them?" "Because they already had heating in them." "Why was the heating not upgraded?" "Because it met the minimum requirement." "So, because it met the minimum requirement, you were happy that it was sufficient and were not prepared to spend anymore?" "Well, yes," answered Nick sheepishly. He just realised that he sounded like a miser rather than a businessman. It didn't help that Amanda gave him a 'I told you so' look. Brian took his pen and wrote 'meets minimum requirement' down on the whiteboard next to the list. "Now, for the last one. Why is the rent so high?" "It is comparable for the area." Nick replied defensively. "Why is it comparable?" "Because, that is what the other houses around the area go for." "Why is the rent that good for the other houses?" "Because they are good houses on good streets." It suddenly dawned on Nick that his houses were not of the same standard as the other houses in the area where he invested. "Before you continue, I know what the root cause is. I have charged for a property that does not match the quality of the same type of houses in the area." Brian wrote down 'house does not match the quality of surrounding houses'. They looked over the list as Brian finished writing.

1. Shabby property – Financial Freedom

2. Wrong tenant – No model to pass on to the agent

3. Energy performance too low – Minimum requirement

4. Rent too high – House does not match the quality of the surrounding houses

"Where do we go from here?" asked Amanda. "We need to come up with counter-measures for each of these things and assign the person who will be responsible for getting it done, and so we don't lose sight of it, we need to make it visible." Brian once again took the marker pen and began to draw lines and put headings on the whiteboard.

No	Problem	Counter-measure	Responsible	Date	Status
1	Shabby house	Internal refurbishment	Nick	6/6/16	Open
2	No Model for agent	Document to inform agent	Amanda	7/3/16	Open
3	Poor Energy performance	Double glazing and home insulation	Nick	6/5/16	Open
4	Poor quality house	Refurbishment to high standard and kerb appeal	Amanda	6/6/16	Open

"Now, we can see what the countermeasure is, who is responsible, the date that it should be completed by and the current status. By making it visible and having daily meetings to discuss it will ensure we stay focused and if there is a problem, we can deal with it at an early stage. Remember, this is a top-level view. Below this, you will have a list of things to do to meet the counter-measures; for example, for the internal refurbishment, you need to ensure that the trades are working to a high standard and they have not cut corners on anything, and you will have a snagging list." "This is a pretty good idea; I can see the merit of doing this as we will keep each other on our toes." Nick was really enthusiastic for the first time during this process as he could see the possibilities of using this method in his business. Amanda was happy to see Nick taking an interest and she had a feeling that things will get better in their business. "Just one question, shouldn't numbers one and four go together?" Nick asked. Brian smiled before answering. "That would be like inspecting your own work, whereas by making Amanda responsible, she will make sure that the materials that you use and the standardisation of the kitchens, bathroom etc. will be of a good quality but is also practical, and of course, you are not going to argue with her." "Too right he won't." They all laughed at Amanda's quip. Brian checked his watch, "I think that we have time to talk about the tenant that you want. So, what would your ideal tenant be like?" Nick and Amanda made suggestions and Brian wrote them down.

1. Long standing

2. Look after the property

3. Law abiding

4. Professionals

"Right, now what makes the tenant want to remain at your property?" "Having a good quality home," ventured Nick. "What else?" "I can't think of anything else at the moment." "Me neither." "What about being suitable for a family and being near a good school for their children to attend? They may also want to be near family and friends as they will want to be close to the area that they were brought up in as that is where they are most happy." Nick flinched as he could not help but think of his parents when Brian brought this point up. Amanda watched Nick out of the corner of her eye to see how he would react, but she needn't have worried as he seemed lost in thought. "You say that you want professionals, but these tend to move around every couple of years if they are career-minded, so look for professionals with a family as they may stay longer. Also, consider people who claim benefits but are actively looking for work. These people may have just fallen on some bad times but they tend to try and pick themselves up again, so don't dismiss them. Also, in this group, consider the disabled people who receive benefits for although they may not work, the local councils will help with your refurbishment and you will have a long-term tenant and of course, you will have the feel good factor for helping them. The third set of people to look at is ex-military people. I have a friend who came out of the forces and wanted to rent a house but was unemployed. He could not claim anything because he had no fixed address, so he was caught up in no man's land. I ended up putting him up for a month until he could get all of his paperwork sorted out, which allowed him to get a house to rent and sort out employment. You couldn't ask for a better type of tenant as they keep your property clean and spotless as this is a habit from the forces and they will look after your property as well as be law abiding." "I never gave them a thought before now; they just don't come to mind when it comes to renting," Nick admitted. "Perhaps we could contact the military about people who want to rent as there may be an association or something similar that could help us with this," suggested Amanda. "That's a great idea; I think that you and

Nick should follow up on this. Now that you have come up with the bones of the type of tenant you want, I suggest that you put this into a document and present it to your agent for them to follow as this will be your standards." It had been a long day and they had covered a lot of ground. Nick was feeling exhausted, not only from having to think about his business whenever Brian asked a question, but he was also emotionally drained from thinking about his parents as he was being questioned; it was not something he had been prepared for. "Do you mind if we call it a day Brian?" Brian checked his watch, "I think we have done enough for today, but I do want you to do some homework and make a start on the ideal tenant document for your agent." Amanda agreed as Brian tidied up and got ready to leave. Amanda showed him out and went back to check on Nick. "Are you ok?" "Sure, just a bit exhausted after a day of lots of concentration." Amanda could see that there was more to it than that but she did not know how to approach the subject without making Nick defensive as this would result in an argument, so she kept quiet and hoped that Nick would open up. Nick heard the quietness in the room and felt compelled to fill the void. "Today has made me think more about the tenant needs." "In what way?" He hesitated for a moment. "I guess it's about them feeling happy in the property and being near family and friends." Amanda gently nudged him on. "Go on." Nick was reluctant to continue. Suddenly, his emotions got the better of him and his pent up feelings flooded out. "It has brought my parents to mind; I have treated my parents really badly. They have always been there for me and encouraged me and instead of being thankful, I was an arrogant little shit, who thought he knew better and because I didn't get my own way, I just walked away from my parents and completely disowned them. Instead of trying to move them away from their home into somewhere they did not want to live in, I should have gone to the council and just bought their house for them under the right to buy scheme. I just did not think of it at the time. I also did not tell them anything about you and refused to let them come to our wedding, and now I regret everything that I did to them." Nick choked up and his eyes were watery as he tried to hold back the tears. Amanda went over to him and hugged him. She gave him a moment. "Why don't you contact them?" Amanda suggested. Nick shook his head. "The way that I have treated them, they would not want anything to do with me." "You don't know that Nick, you have to make an effort, or you will live to regret this for the rest of your life." "I'll think about it." Amanda decided not to push Nick further as he had come a long way and she did not want him to go back to being stubborn and defensive. He had to come to terms with his emotions in his own time.

Chapter Four

Amanda went to work on the document to give to her lettings agent to let them know what type of tenant they were excepting in their property. It took her a little while before she was happy with her result and she showed it to Nick.

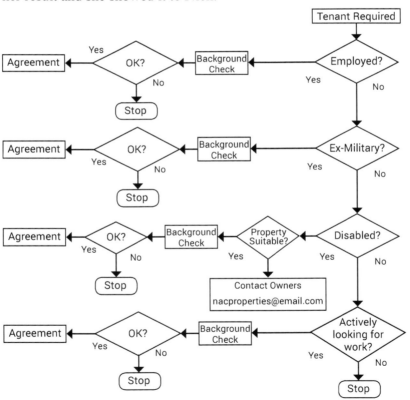

Nick looked over Amanda's work and was impressed. He had not thought of producing a decision map for agents to use as a guide when choosing tenants for their properties. "This is a great job! It's clear so there should be no misunderstandings." Amanda was very pleased with Nick's reaction to her work. More importantly, she recognised that documenting things in this format would make her life much easier when she managed the agents, as they could make the majority of the decisions by using the model and the only part that she needed to get involved in is if she got an email about a property that was not suitable for someone who was disabled in its current form.

Brian arrived at the house and was ushered into the living room by Amanda. As soon as he was sat down, Amanda presented him with her tenant model. As Brian looked through it, Amanda informed Nick that Brian had arrived as she went off to prepare a drink for all of them. As they sipped their drinks, Brian complimented Amanda on her good work, and she beamed at his praise. It almost felt like being in school again when she was praised for getting top marks by her teacher. She loved that feeling then and to her surprise, she found that she enjoyed the same attention now. "I am curious, what happens if you need to get a tenant out for whatever reason?" "Well, the law states that we have to serve them a notice, but they could still drag it on and it could go to court, which is costly; or they can wreck the place too, so it is not something we do lightly." Nick agreed with Amanda. Brian thought about the situation for a minute before asking another question. "What if you were to ask for a guarantor for each of your tenants?" A light just went off in Nick's head. "Blow me down, why didn't I think of that? That would save us time and money because if anything happened to the house, we could go after the guarantor, who does not have the protection that a tenant has, so they would ensure that everything is in good order. We need to add that as part of the tenancy agreement, as no guarantor would sign an agreement if they did not have confidence that the tenant would behave and keep the property in good order." Nick was grinning like a Cheshire cat at the thought of not being at the mercy of the tenant. "Well if we get your property and business right, you should not have to worry about getting tenants out of your properties." Amanda agreed with Brian. "They are still a problem," Nick persisted. "I thought the same way as you Nick until Trevor pointed out that it is the system that allows the person to make mistakes, so you need to fix the system. This is why we started with the SIPOC diagram and agreed that most of your problems can be fixed by looking at the processes within the system. In your case, you see the tenant as the problem, but the reality is that, it is your system, which in this case, it is your property that needs fixing. If you get your property right and to a high standard and you get your rent right, your tenant will be happy to live there." Nick frowned. "Hun, you need to see it from the tenant's point of view and not ours. You know as well as I do that we have skimped on things just to save a little bit of money and we have ended up getting voids, so let's do things properly and see how much of a difference it will make." Nick conceded. He knew they were right. He had to change his mind-set from seeing the tenant as a problem, because he knew that without them, they would not have a business. "What shall we do next?" Amanda asked, eager to get on. "We can put together a simple dashboard so that we can track each of your properties without having to go through all of the records. This will be top level but it will help you have a quick overview of your properties." "That sounds good to me," replied Nick. Brian quickly went to work on an excel spreadsheet where he created tabs that he hyperlinked so that he could click through with ease and not have to find the correct tab. Nick and Amanda watched as Brian worked; he made it look so easy! "Well, here is the basic home page, you can add houses as you populate the spreadsheet. For now and for simplicity, I have called it house number one, you can change the name to make it more meaningful to you." Nick and Amanda looked over his shoulder as he was explaining it.

"So now when you click on it, you will be taken to the house basic tab." Brian clicked on House 1 and was taken to the tab.

"Here, you have the basic details of the house, and if you click on the headings that are in blue, they will take you to the relevant tab. If you click on your logo at the top, it will take you to your home page." Brian clicked on the 'Rent per Month Post Cost' heading and was taken to the correct tab.

He then clicked on the logo and it took him back to the home page. Nick and Amanda were very impressed and could see the benefit of using the dashboard, as it would give them a quick overview of their properties. "That's great Brian; I can cross reference this to our files so that I know which file I need to look at when I am calling up a property, which will make my job much easier." Amanda was really happy. "That is a good idea Amanda. It also means that I don't have to try and find the information or bug you to find it for me." "Glad that you both like this idea; this is just a small step to help you eliminate waste from your system." Amanda was suddenly interested. "What do you mean by waste?" she asked. "I'm glad that you asked as this would be a good time to introduce you to what is known as the seven wastes." Nick was very curious. "I have never heard of the seven wastes before; where has that come from?" "Ok, history lesson coming up. This began with the car manufacturer, Toyota; they created this because they did not have much money in comparison to their automotive manufacturing competitors, so they had to be creative and find ways to make the most of what they had and optimise all of their processes from the shop floor to the office, so they looked at eliminating as much waste as possible. In order to eliminate the waste, they first had to identify and define what waste meant to them, so they come up with the seven wastes." Brian took out his whiteboard pen and began to write on the board. "Here are the seven wastes."

1. Transport

2. Inventory

3. Motion

4. Waiting

5. Over Processing

6. Over Production

7. Defects

"These can be remembered by using the acronym *TIMWOOD*. Now, I will explain what each of these wastes mean and how it can be applied to your business. We will begin with transport. This means the movement of material from one location to another. In your case, it could mean that you view individual properties in several different areas, so you can have a lot of traveling in between properties. The traveling that you do has no added value and costs you in fuel and time, so you can try and eliminate some of this transport by viewing a larger number of properties within the same area. Also, there is the question of the suppliers of your refurbishment materials; if they are too far away, you are paying extra cost for transport and it will cost you if you have to return something or need to see them for any reason, whereas if you source the suppliers in the same area, or if you have a national supplier that has local branches, this will cut down on transportation." Nick was thoughtful. "This is true," he thought, "we do waste an awful lot of time flitting from area to area." "So, what you're saying is that, we should not use a shotgun approach to investing and become more focused in specific areas?" asked Amanda. "You have hit the nail on the head, so you and Nick need to think about your investment areas." "But we already have properties in several different areas so how do we cut down on travelling to these?" Nick asked. "If you have properties far and wide and you need to visit them, or the agents in these areas, I suggest that you make it a road trip, and maybe combine it with a few days' holiday in some of the areas. That way, you're not having to come home each time in between trips." "That's a good idea and it also means that we get a break too Hun." Nick couldn't disagree with Amanda, as it had been a while since they had had a break, as they never seemed to have time to go on holiday. "The next waste is inventory. This is classed as work in progress or finished goods that have not been sold yet. When we apply this to your business, it is the cost of having a property refurbished or a property that is empty or not sold. There are other inventories within this; for instance, you may have horded a number of items from refurbishments as a 'just in case something gets broken'." Amanda gave Nick a knowing look, as Nick coloured up a little with embarrassment. "We do have two garages full of stuff." Nick admitted sheepishly. "The majority could probably be sold off online so you could at least make some money from it. Just keep a small amount of what is truly required as spares. It would also mean that you could possibly free up both garages which could then either be rented out or sold." "You mentioned that a refurbishment is an inventory; I don't see how we can reduce that waste, after all, a refurbishment is a refurbishment." "Well Amanda, what we can do in this instance is to reduce the time it takes to complete and get the property filled. I will go into that when we start the refurb of your Nuneaton property." Amanda was satisfied with Brian's answer and could not wait to get started on that property. "Now, I will talk about motion. Traditionally, this means excessive travel between workstations either by people or machines. In your business, it could be that, your files are at floor level in boxes rather than at waist level labelled up on a shelf so that there easily retrievable. The same goes for things like your printer paper. Whilst talking about printers, it may be a case that your printer is outside of your working area, so you have to go to it to retrieve your documents, so think about how much travelling you do to retrieve things in your work area." This seemed simple and straightforward, so Nick asked Brian to go onto the next waste. "Ok, our next waste is waiting. In an organisation, this could mean waiting for an answer from another department. This can apply to your business; for instance, Amanda creates a document and gives it to you Nick to review, but you decide that you will review it later as you are far too busy. It means that Amanda cannot issue that document, so everything is held up." Amanda agreed that this was often the case between them, as each of them looked after different parts of the business. "The same applies to your suppliers. Your refurbishment could be held up because they haven't delivered on time, and some of it could also be up to you, as you have not planned ahead." "What do you mean by that?" asked Nick. "Suppose that you wanted a particular kitchen for your property. You place your order whilst forgetting to ask what the lead-time is to obtain the kitchen. So now, you are full swing into the refurbishment and want the kitchen only to be told that it is not available for another two weeks. So, you get mad at your supplier and blame them for poor customer service, when in fact the fault is yours for not planning things and not working with your supplier." Nick and Amanda nodded in agreement. This sort of thing had happened in the past, and they had even vowed not to use a supplier because of it, and now they could see it was not the supplier's fault, the blame was on them. "We spend a lot of time in both our business life as well as our personal life waiting for things, so the more we can eliminate through good system planning, the more time will be freed up for us to do other things." "So, by eliminating waiting, we are in fact creating good time management." "Correct Nick, that is exactly what we are doing. This leads us to one of the most serious of wastes: over producing. In manufacturing terms, this would mean large batch quantities being made which leads to high levels of inventory. In your business, this could mean duplication of documents: both of you working on the same thing in isolation of each other, placing duplicate orders with suppliers etc. All of these things not only cost you time and money but can also lead to arguments and stress. Your aim is to do things once and exactly when you need it. This is known as 'just in time' or 'JIT' for short. You should not be doing things on a 'just in case' principle, which is what most companies do." Nick and Amanda understood this waste only too well as they have argued over when they had duplicated tasks and then blamed each other for it and at times. When the arguments had been over a major purchase, it had not been pretty, and they had had to sort out the mess with the supplier to return the goods. "That has happened to us a few times, so we know where you're coming from with this," said Nick. "Right, in that case, I will move on to the next waste which is over processing. From a manufacturing standpoint, this could be over engineering a part, so although it does the job, the extra cost does not add value. Applying this to property, it could be that you have multi coloured walls instead of one colour, or that you hang a door with four hinges when two would suffice. An example in your business would be that before you make a decision on anything, you want every document, all the analysis, consult with people etc. In the meantime, because of the delay in making up your mind, the deal is gone." "What you're talking about in this case is analysis paralysis, is it not?" asked Nick "Yes, it is Nick, so think about how you can eliminate this waste from your business, as this is not an easy one. People get caught up in wanting to know everything instead of making a decision." "Thinking about it, you're right. Nick and I have lost some deals because we have hummed and hared over it because we wanted more details rather than taking action." "Every business does this at some point; you just need to be mindful. The last waste and the most obvious but one of the hardest to detect before it gets to your customer is defects. In your business, this is usually found in documentation and of course in the property itself. Therefore, you need to find a way to detect it first, as this will cause you and your customer less problems or better still, prevent it from happening in the first place. This is why we need to look at standard work as this reduces the risk of having defects in the first place, and every time you come across a defect, have the discipline to go through the root cause analysis so that you can bottom it out and put a corrective action in place to prevent it from happening again." "Putting it simply, what you are saying is that, if we can remove all of the defects, then our business will run smoothly, and our tenants will be happy." "Yes Nick, that is exactly what I am saying, and if you do that with all of the wastes in your system, then you will have a world-class business." "It is a lot to think about when you are trying to run a business, how do you keep on top of it?" asked Amanda. "There is a technique that Deming used called *Plan Do Check Act* or *PDCA*. He learnt it from his mentor, Walter A. Shewhart. By using this technique to look at each part of your business, you will find the problems and eliminate them. This is what the model looks like." Brian took his pen and began to draw. Nick and Amanda watched over his shoulder as he drew a circle which he then divided into four quadrants and wrote a title in each of the quadrants. He then drew some arrows around the outside.

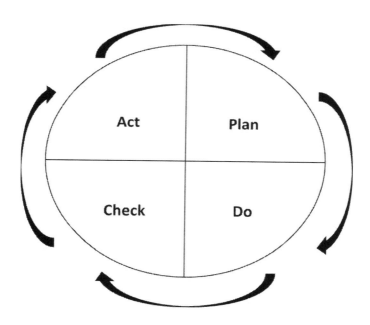

"We start with Plan as this is our objective based on the target that we want to achieve. By establishing an expected target, we will know if we have achieved the desired results." "How would we pick a target?" Nick wanted to know. "The target could be something that you want to achieve within the business such as standard work for all of your processes or it could be something major such as growing your business by having another thirty properties within two years." "So, there is no limit to this model?" Amanda asked. "No, you can make your target as big or as small as you like. The model can even be used in such a way that it is interactive with each other.

Let me explain. You can have a number of small targets that when complete, feeds into a bigger target. For example, if we use PDCA to eliminate waste, it could feed into the bigger target of cutting down costs whilst still producing growth. Do you understand what I mean?" Both Nick and Amanda nodded and agreed that they did, so Brian went on to the next quadrant in the model. "Once we have established our target in planning, we move on to the Do phase. This is where we plan on what we want to look at to be able to achieve our target. We then collect the data and information to understand what we need to do when we go into the following stages of the model." This was clearly understood by Nick and Amanda, so Brian moved on to explain the Check part of the model. "Once you have gathered the relative data and information, you can then check it and compare it against your stated target. What you are looking for is the gap between what you currently have, to where you want to be with your target. Any differences or deviations need to be noted as this gap needs to be filled." "You mention information and data, what do you mean by that?" asked Nick. "Information could mean that when you look through your documentation, you find that you have several documents that are duplicated but have different contents, such as the tenancy agreements that you have, or that you find that there should have been a document in place that you had forgotten to create such as a guide to living in shared accommodation for your HMO's. The data could be house price trends for a particular area that you are investing in, or the number of voids that you have had in all of your properties. Remember, the data and information you collect must be relevant to your objectives." "Ok, that makes sense."

"From there, we move onto the next part of the cycle which is Act. This is where you put things in place to close the gap that you have discovered; this will then become your new baseline. You need this new baseline to settle so as to ensure that it is working, and then you go around the cycle again to see if your new baseline meets the target. If it does, then you can close this issue, but if it doesn't meet the target, you need to go around the Plan Do Check Act cycle again until it does." "So, this model gets you to think about your target and then forces you to look at all aspects of your business to hit that target by making you check and recheck until it hits the target. This is very powerful, why don't they teach you these things at school, as I can see the benefit in any situation from learning to business?" Amanda observed. Nick was in agreement with Amanda. "I can see that it can be used for short-term goals as well as long-term goals." "You are both right, this is a method of ensuring continuous improvement of your system which will keep your business healthy. If you don't keep changing, you will start to get stuck in a rut an eventually, you will be left behind by your competitors. As Albert Einstein once said, the definition of insanity is doing the same thing over and over again and expecting a different result." They had been so engrossed with the work that they did not realise how much time they had spent until Amanda started feeling peckish and looked at her watch. "Bloody hell, it's five o'clock, I should have made us some lunch ages ago!" she exclaimed. Brian told her not to worry about it. The main thing is that, it had been a fruitful day as they had learnt on how to work on their business rather than be in their business. He told them to think about all of the things they had discussed and start to apply them. He informed them that he would not be seeing them for a few weeks as he had to get back to the office for a meeting and to catch up with his own business. He promised he would give them a call to let them know when he was available. They said their goodbyes and Brian left to head off home.

Chapter Five

Brian was in his office just checking his diary when he received a phone call from the planner. "Hello Susan, I take it that you have some news for me?" He listened as Susan told him that they had received planning permission to convert the loft in the property. Brian was delighted; he knew that if anyone could get planning permission, it would be Susan. She knew all the council planners all over the country and she was tenacious and persuasive and always got her way so long as she was brought in at the start of the process and before the architects got in on the act. He thanked her and told her that her fee would be transferred to her account within the next half hour. Brian made a habit of paying his suppliers quickly as he knew they were usually short of cash as the bigger clients put in payment clauses that could mean that they did not get paid for anytime between thirty and ninety days. By doing this, he always received good service; he knew that there were times when suppliers were really busy but they would somehow always make room for him. He also got a lot of inside information on his competitors. They used the same suppliers so he would get little snippets such as who was buying more or less or going to a different service or picked up a big job. He found this very useful, which is why he worked very closely with his suppliers. Brian then rang Nick to tell him the good news. "Hi Nick, we have planning permission to do the loft conversion. I have paid her for the work, so I will send over the invoice. Do you have an architect you usually use?" Nick replied that he shopped around until he found one that could do the job cheaply. Brian was not surprised by the answer as he had come to expect this from Nick. "Ok Nick, as with other suppliers, we are going to find a good architect and we are going to work closely with them and use them for all of your properties, so we are going to need someone who not only is good at their job, but also someone that you can get along with." Nick agreed so Brian arranged to meet up with Nick and Amanda in a couple of days' time.

"Morning Brian." Amanda was very cheerful as she opened the door for him and led him through to the now familiar living room rather than the office. Nick was already seated and waiting for him and whilst Brian sat and made himself comfortable, Amanda poured out a cup of coffee for him. They had a general chat to catch up whilst they sipped their drinks. "Ok, down to business. Have you used any architect on a regular basis?" Nick and Amanda looked at each other as they both thought about it. "No, I can't recall using the same one twice, can you Hun?" Nick agreed with Amanda that they had not used a regular architect. "We will have to find one that suits your needs as not all architects are the same." "I thought that so long as they were qualified architects, they could draw up plans for any job that they were given." "No Nick. Unfortunately, that is not the case. You see architects can specialise in different types of buildings such as listed buildings, or commercial buildings, and of course, some are more creative than others. Therefore, if you get the wrong architect, not only will you be disappointed but also it can be an expensive mistake." "How come you know so much about architects?" asked Amanda. Brian cleared his throat before he answered. "When I wanted a new office, I looked around for an architect based on price and commissioned an architect that was cheap. He sounded like he knew what he was talking about, and of course, I trusted him to deliver. How wrong I was! He had only previously worked on small houses for council social housing, a notion I was not aware of, and here I was commissioning him to work on his first commercial building. Well, to cut the long story short, he made numerous mistakes, which caused delays and cost me a lot of money as it went over budget and the final result was disappointing to say the least. I used it for several years, as I did not have the funds to make the necessary changes. Eventually, after the business had really taken off, I looked around for an architect that specialised in commercial buildings and found one that really understood my needs and he designed my current office. He was not cheap, but he did save me a lot of money, as he was also creative. Anyone that walks into my office cannot help but be impressed, and my employees are happy to work there as it is comfortable, airy and has lots of natural light." "Where do we start?" asked Nick. "We can start by asking friends, neighbours, colleagues etc. for recommendations as these people have had a form of experience, one way or another. If that does not go through, you can look up the Architects Registration Board on the internet as under UK law, all practicing architects must be registered with the board. The board ensures that architects are not only well trained through checking up on them, but also that they have professional indemnity insurance so that if there is a compensation claim against them, they are covered. There is also the Royal Institute of British Architects, which is a voluntary trade association, and their members are called chartered architects. What you will then do is draw up a shortlist of the architects that you think will fit your bill and give them a brief of the work that you require along with a rough budget. You will then narrow down that list to no more than three architects then have an in-depth discussion with them about the project. Ask to see their portfolios and speak to their previous clients. Visit their website and if possible, go and visit the houses that they have done, and then pick the architect that you want to work with." "That sounds like such a drawn-out process just to get an architect," Nick observed. "It is, but it will pay dividends in the long term, and remember, there could also be a delay in getting them to do the work as the best architects are in demand so the sooner you start this process the better." "So, our project could be delayed?" Nick asked. "I'm afraid so. That is why it is important that you get moving on this." "I will get on it straight away," piped up Amanda before Nick could make any other objections.

Brian was thankful that Amanda stepped in as it prevented Nick from raising objections that may have ended up in an argument as he could see that Amanda was keen on making the changes to their business and he did not want her discouraged in any way. "To help you in communicating with all concerned parties of the project, I will show you a matrix that is known by its acronym *RACI*. This stands for Responsible, Accountable, Consulted, Informed. In fact, this matrix can be used in all parts of your business as it is a very powerful and useful tool." Nick and Amanda quickly became interested. Brian started to draw a grid and added titles.

	Responsible	Accountable	Consulted	Informed

"Right. Along the side, we put our issues and then we decide who is responsible, who is accountable, who needs to be consulted and who needs to be informed. Let's create an example so that you can understand it better." With that, Brian started to fill out the matrix to show Nick and Amanda how it works.

	Responsible	Accountable	Consulted	Informed
Produce Plans	Architect	Nick & Amanda	Dave the Builder	Brian (Project Manager)
Approve Plans	Nick & Amanda	Architect	Dave the Builder	Brian (Project Manager)
Start Build	Dave the Builder	Brian (Project Manager)	Architect	Nick & Amanda

"I don't get this; shouldn't the architect be accountable for the plans?" asked Amanda. "I think I had better explain the roles of each of these so that you really understand it beginning with Responsible. This is the person who does the actual work and achieves the task.

The person who is Accountable is normally the project sponsor and ensures that the project is completed and approves the work. The person or people as it can be more than one person who is consulted are usually subject matter experts and will normally provide information for the task or project, and finally Informed are the people that need to be told about the task as these people could be affected by the outcome, so they need to be kept informed of the progress. I hope that this now makes sense to you." "I get it now; I understand why we are accountable for the plans. This is a good visual tool as I can see who does what for each task at a glance, so I know who I need to see when I want to know something." Amanda was very enthusiastic. Nick was nodding in agreement. "I can also see why you said it can be used in any part of the business. It really is a very powerful tool, and I am so glad that you showed it to us." Nick agreed. "You're welcome; I am glad that you have understood it and appreciate that it can be used in your business."

The morning had passed so quickly. Amanda noted the time, as she was not going to be caught up in it as she had on Brian's last visit. "Time for a spot of lunch I think. Ham salad baguette and a coffee ok with you Brian? Amanda asked. Brian glanced at his watch before answering. "Yes, that will be fine, thank you." Nick excused himself and went off to his office to check his emails and Brian rang his office to check in and see if he was needed. Ten minutes later, they were sitting out on the patio enjoying the sun and some fresh air as they ate. As they were sipping their drinks, Amanda decided to ask Brian a question. "I was thinking about the waste that we talked about the last time you were here. Is there a way that we can identify these wastes easily?" Brian thought about it for a minute. "I guess the easiest way for you would be to produce a process map as this is another visual tool that can help you." Nick was attentive as Amanda replied. "Can you show us what you mean as I have never heard of a process map before." "Sure, as soon as we have finished lunch and get back inside, we can construct a map so that you can see what it looks like." Amanda couldn't wait as she found all of these tools and techniques useful and she could see it would help their business. Nick was equally enthusiastic, but he tended to play it down a bit, as he did not want to come across like a kid with a new toy. They finished their lunch, gathered up the cups and plates, and put them in the kitchen on their way to the lounge. Brian took a whiteboard pen and began to draw a simple layout.

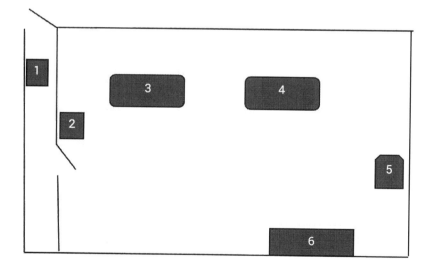

"Ok, here is a simple layout that represents your office. Number one is the hallway table, number two is the office table, number three is Nick's desk, number four is Amanda's desk, number five is the printer/scanner and number six is the filing cabinet. Now, let us assume that you have had some post that needs attention. So now, we will add this to the map in the form of a trail that it will follow." Brian began adding some lines to the map.

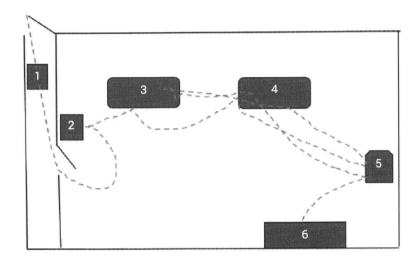

"The post arrives and is placed on the hall table, then half an hour later, it gets placed on the office table. Nick then comes along, picks it up, and takes it to his desk where he opens it and then decides it's something that Amanda needs to deal with, so he puts it on Amanda's desk. Amanda then reads it and has to respond, so she types up a letter and prints it out. Amanda then retrieves the letter from the printer and gives it to Nick to sign. Nick reads through it and then signs it and passes it back to Amanda. Amanda then goes

"If we remove the two little tables, it will eliminate two hand offs. Therefore, the post will go directly to Nick's desk. We have moved the printer in between you as you have suggested." "There is no travel to the filing cabinet," Nick observed. "You are correct. If you are scanning the paperwork, why do you need to file it? Your paperwork would be kept on your computer and backed up on a cloud-based system or on a separate external hard drive. We can reduce the waste even further." Brian made some more changes to the diagram.

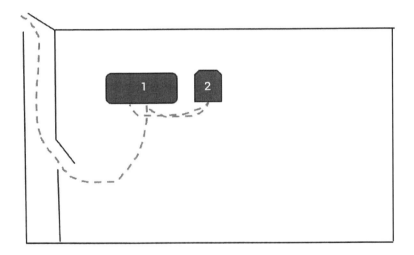

"The post goes directly to Nick's desk where Nick processes it, so this eliminates the hand off to Amanda." That sounds good to me; from now on Nick, you can do all of the work." Nick smiled good humouredly as he replied, "I don't think so; this is about teamwork, and so you will have to pull your weight too." "Now, we will look at a process map with swim lanes. It is used mainly where we have a number of functions or people and we want to show the interactions between them. I am going to draw for you an actual process map that Trevor put together for a company." "How will you remember what Trevor did?" Amanda asked. Brian smiled to himself as he remembered how this map came about. "This was a company that I was working with and Trevor came to have a look at what I was doing as part of my business. Well, as we were in the assets office, Trevor suddenly began observing what was going on and checking his watch. I could see he was engaged and so I didn't disturb him and just watched what he was doing. After what seemed like quite a long time, he suddenly said that there was a lot of waste in this process. The owner of the company just happened to be there and heard Trevor's comment, so he challenged him on it. Trevor smiled and told him that he would gladly show him, so he had me and the asset team prepare the process map. At the time, none of us knew how to produce a process map so it was a learning curve for all of us. We produced the map and Trevor proved his point. It showed the owner how much waste there was in the system." Amanda was satisfied with Brian's reply, so Brian picked some coloured pens and drew some lines. "These lines are called swim lanes, as they are similar to competitive swimming where each swimmer has their own lane," Brian explained as he continued to colour within the swim lanes. He then used Post-it® notes to complete the swim lanes. "This map shows the process for the Service Charge Budget".

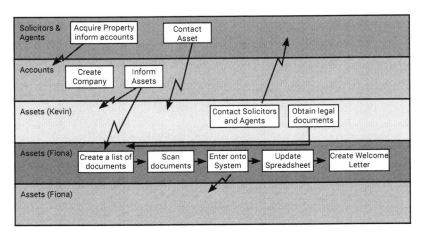

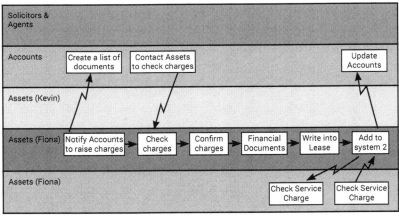

"What are those squiggly arrows for?" Amanda asked. "Those are electronic communications. What stands out on this map?" Nick and Amanda reviewed the map. "Work is mostly being done by one person, even though there are three people in the department." "You are right Nick. Now, how long do you think it took to create the Service Charge Budget?" "About two hours?" "I think that it took a bit longer, maybe three hours," suggested Amanda. "You are both completely wrong; this process took two thousand one hundred and ninety minutes or thirty-six and a half hours." Nick and Amanda were completely shocked, and Brian was amused to see the expressions on their faces. "No way!" exclaimed Nick. "That was the owner's exact reaction; he went over it again with the team and questioned everything, but it was correct, as they had followed all the written procedures which we pinned on the map as reference. The owner then asked Trevor to look into all of his company's processes as he realised that he had a lot of waste and he needed it fixed. The person doing most of the work was really happy as she had been saying for quite some time that she was overworked and was drowning in paperwork." "Wow, I bet that was an eye opener for the company owner." "Yes, it was Amanda, and I learnt a lot from it too as I was working closely with Trevor on this project and applied a lot of what I had learnt to my own business." "How long did it take to remove the waste from the business?" Nick asked. "Trevor and I worked with them for six months; we not only removed the waste in the company but Trevor also trained the staff so that they could learn how to do it for themselves so that they only call him in if they really get stuck." Amanda was curious, "so, how long did this particular process take after you made the improvements?" "We got that down to three and a half hours by the time we left. The company thought that they could reduce it further, so they were going to work on it after the system was in place, so it could be less now." "Thirty-three hours is a huge saving, both in time and money." "Yes it is Nick, that is why I am keen that you map out your processes, you may be shocked at the amount of time you waste that could be put to better use." "I can see that now; it looks like we have a lot of homework to do." He sighed. Amanda nodded in agreement, but the thought was a little bit daunting. "Cheer up you two, it's not that bad. Start off with your smallest and easiest process and work your way up to the complex ones. If you do that, not only will you have some quick hits, but you will also learn how to do these maps and soon, it will become second nature to you, and by the time you get to the really complex staff, you will do it without it scaring you." "I suppose you are right, and it would help us to understand our business." "We can do this Hun, and if it can help us do things quicker and better, then it's got to be a good thing." "As always, you're right, we can do this." Brian was glad that their enthusiasm had returned, as he did not want them to slip back; they had to keep their momentum going. He looked at his watch. "I guess we can call it a day, you have plenty to get on with, but your priority should be sorting out your architect. Give me a call when you have found one." Nick and Amanda thanked Brian for his help and Amanda showed him out and waved as he drove off.

Chapter Six

Nick and Amanda did as Brian had suggested and contacted the people they knew to see if they had any dealings with architects or could recommend one. One of Nick's contacts from a property network gave him a name of an architect that he had used for a project. Nick asked if it was possible for him to view the property in question to which his contact agreed, so they made arrangements to meet up at the property. Nick pulled up in his car outside the address he had been given and he realised that it was quite a large three-story building. He sat in his car for about ten minutes before his contact showed up. Nick got out to meet him. "Hi Rob, thank you for taking the time to show me your property," Nick said as he shook hands with Rob. "You're welcome Nick, glad that I could be of help. Right, let's get in so that you can have a general look around." Rob led the way and opened the front door; it became immediately apparent to Nick that this was a HMO as the rooms had fire doors. "This is an eight-bedroom HMO," proudly said Rob. This confirmed what Nick had suspected. "We can have a look around the common areas, and I can show you one of the rooms as the tenant has just vacated it, as his company has promoted him and moved him to another site." "So, these are professional lets then?" "Yes, they are. That is why the house is clean and tidy and I do not get any problems." Nick and Rob wandered around the house as Rob pointed out the changes that had been made. From what Nick could see; the standard of work was very good. "How long did it take to convert it to a HMO?" "This took nine months from start to finish." Nick was impressed considering the work that had to be done to convert it to a HMO, but still decided to ask a question about it. "So, was that on plan?" "No, we had estimated that it would take no more than six months, but building work was slow as the trades had to work around each other." "Was it on budget?" "Again no, we went over budget by fifteen thousand pounds, due to the delays that I have just mentioned." "Ouch, that hurts." "Yes, it did at the time and it gave me a few sleepless nights, but I am happy with the results and this property's current cash flow, so it was worth it in the end." They finished their tour of the property and bid each other farewell.

"How was it?" Amanda asked. "I was impressed with the work, but a little worried that it went three months over the planned time and fifteen thousand pounds over budget." "Nick, stop being so negative. We have Brian as our project manager and from what we have seen so far, I'm sure that he will cut the waste down to a bare minimum," she admonished. "Yes, you are right dear, I guess old habits die hard. Well, it looks like we may have found our architect as the layout and the use of space and light was really good." Amanda was pleased as she wanted to work like this from the start, but Nick was always cautious and sometimes Nick's penny-pinching ways infuriated her, so it was good that he was starting to listen. Nick was tempted to go with just the one architect, but Amanda would not hear of it. She pointed out to him that it was pointless listening to

Brian's advice if they were not going to follow it, so with reluctance, Nick made more enquires on his network. Four more architects were recommended to him and again, he arranged for him and Amanda to visit each of the properties and was equally impressed with the work that he had seen. He now felt like he was in a bit of a dilemma, as he did not know which one to choose. Nick and Amanda talked it over and decided that they needed Brian's guidance to help them make the choice. Nick called Brian and explained the situation. "Nick, I am out of the country at the moment just finishing a deal for another project and won't be back until next week, but I will get my office to email you a form that you can use." "Thank you Brian, that would be great!" "No problem Nick, and when I get back, we can arrange to meet up and go through the replies as hopefully, the architects will have responded by then." A few hours later, Nick received an email with an attachment from Brian's office, which Nick quickly opened, downloaded, and printed so that he and Amanda could review it before sending it off to the architect.

Architect Enquiry Form

Name:		Company:	
Address:			
Tel:	Mobile:	Email:	Web Address:
Project Detail:			
Budget:		Expected completion date of the project:	
What is expected from the architect?			
Part B to be completed by the Architect			
Name:		Company:	
Address:			
ARB No:	Tel:	Email:	Web Address:

Architect Fee:	How are the fees calculated, and are there any extra costs?
When can you start?	What other information do you need from the owner?
Signature:	Date:

"Well, that seems straight forward; we can get this off to the architects straight away." "I will get on it straight away Hun, while you go and make us some drinks." Amanda smiled sweetly at Nick as she said this. Nick smiled as he shook his head and went off to do as he was told.

They were sipping their coffee when Nick heard the phone in his office ring. He left Amanda to finish her drink as he went off to answer the phone. Amanda was thinking of the jobs that she needed to do when she heard Nick raise his voice in agitation. "Another problem," she thought. That meant she would have to calm Nick down. Twenty minutes later, Nick appeared looking quite angry. "What's wrong?" "What's wrong? It's the bloody government that's wrong." Oh, dear, thought Amanda, Nick is going off on a rant. "What has the government done to make you so angry?" "They are a bunch of bloody, faceless, clueless, idiots changing the laws on property investing without consulting the people that do this day in day out. They go on about how there is going to be a shortage of pensions and when you try and do something about it, like investing in property so that you can have a decent pension, they pull the rug from under you." "It can't be that bad surely." "I am just from speaking to Stephen Latham on the phone. He has a friend who works in the government who has tipped him off on changes to property investment. The government wants to change the tax laws so that we end up paying a lot more tax. We are losing our ten percent wear and tear allowance and there will be a reduction in tax relief on interest paid on borrowing. Not only will we have to pay tax up front but also after trading as every other business does; we are being discriminated against. The government wants to get rid of the smaller private investors as they want more corporate investors, and the intention is to force any small private investor to accept tenants that corporate investors won't because they are on benefits, have a poor credit rating, a history of rent arrears, anti-social behaviour etc." "But that's not fair on those who need social housing and it's not fair to property investors. With the new rules on freezing housing allowances and the new way in which those on benefits are getting their money, it could mean that it will be hard for landlords to get paid." "Exactly! This is a total screw up and it only benefits major investors, and guess what, the people that will benefit are also those that are in politics because all parties have their fingers in the property business as they know it's a good bet. The newspapers ought to look into how many people of all parties are involved in property. The only thing we can do is either pull out of property, which is what the government wants, or raise our rents as this will be the only way we can carry on investing, so it will be our tenants that will bear the brunt of the government's bloody meddling." Amanda grew frustrated and angry as the implications began to sink in. "The government tells us that they want small to medium size businesses to flourish as it supports the economy and brings growth, yet we are treated like second hand citizens, whilst the big corporations get all of the tax breaks. The problem with the big investors is that, if it goes wrong, the government will bail them out because they will have too much to lose in housing stock, jobs, tenants losing their homes etc. It's almost like supermarkets which have taken over everywhere and dictate prices and now, lots of town centres are dead because the small retailers can't compete. I'm frightened Nick, as we could lose our livelihood after all of the hard work that we have put into obtaining our business, the risks that we have had to take with our money, the thousands that we have invested in getting educated to learn about property, logistics, book keeping, etc. and the thousands of pounds that we have put into refurbishing old tired properties and it seems like it is all for nothing. How could they do that to us?" The anger and the frustration was too much and Amanda burst into tears. Nick quickly took her in his arms and comforted her as she sobbed into his shoulder. At this moment in time, Nick felt helpless and didn't know what to say or do.

It had been a hard night for them as neither of them got much sleep from worrying about what was going to happen to them. They were emotionally drained. "Hun, what are we going to do?" Amanda pleaded. Again, Nick felt helpless, as it seemed that his world was crashing down around him, but he knew he had to do something for Amanda's sake. "We proceed with the refurbishment of our property so we can be ready to roll when Brian gets back." "What is the point, especially if we are going to have to sell our property?" "I'm going to call Brian and see what he says." Amanda looked up at Nick as he got up and gave him a slight nod. Nick called Brian and explained what had happened and how Amanda was taking it. Brian told Nick that he did not understand enough about it to suggest a solution, but he would call Trevor. Nick thanked him and then, forcing a smile, told Amanda that Brian was going to talk to Trevor and that everything was going to be alright. Amanda gave him a look of both disbelief and hope. "I'm going to make breakfast for us," Nick announced and quickly went off to the kitchen before Amanda could protest. As Nick started to prepare breakfast, his mobile phone went off and his heart skipped a beat when he saw on the caller I.D. that it was Trevor. He answered his phone and started to explain, but Trevor interrupted him by saying that Brian had already filled him in on what had gone on. Trevor then told him that he happened to be home and was going to call Nick to see if he was available to see him. Nick felt like a weight had been lifted off his shoulders and arranged with Trevor for him to call around in an hour's time. Nick quickly finished preparing breakfast, took it in to the dining room, and shouted out to Amanda that breakfast was ready. Amanda appeared and just flopped down in the chair and began toying with her breakfast. "Eat up dear; Trevor is calling round in about an hour." Amanda looked up and saw in Nick's eyes that he was telling the truth. Habit kicked in and she started to eat her breakfast.

The doorbell rang, and Nick quickly went to the door to let Trevor in. They shook hands and Nick led Trevor to the living room where Amanda was waiting. One glance at her told him that Amanda had not slept properly as there were rings around her eyes and a spark missing from her demeanour. He sat down in the chair opposite Nick and Amanda as they sat on the settee. They leaned forward waiting for him to say something. "Right you two, first things first, let's not have a knee jerk reaction to this news. You are business people and these sort of setbacks happen in all businesses so you have to plan for all eventualities and come up with strategies for risk mitigation." Nick and Amanda perked up and began to sit up straight; this is the reaction that Trevor needed. "Ok, what are your goals?" Trevor watched them as they pondered over his question. He needed them to reengage with the business and have some focus. After about ten minutes, Nick answered, "to have an income so that we can be comfortable." "Give me a figure." Nick hesitated as he did some calculations in his head, "two hundred and fifty thousand per year." "What about you Amanda, what is your goal?" Trevor was determined to bring Amanda into the conversation. Amanda looked up. "I want to live abroad." "Where specifically?" "France or Spain, I'm not really bothered." "Well, it is time you got bothered. Which do you prefer? France or Spain?" Amanda thought about the question and images of both countries popped into her mind. "I like the warmth and atmosphere of Spain, but France is closer, so our children and grandchildren can come and visit us easily as it is just a car drive away." Trevor remained silent. Amanda felt awkward, and she suddenly felt the need to fill the void. "I guess that flights are not expensive, and the kids can be with us in a couple of hours." "So, are you telling me that you would like to live in Spain?" Amanda nodded. "Which part of Spain?" "A town called Almuñécar, in the province of Granada." "Why there?" Amanda started to smile as she talked. "It is a beautiful little town right by the sea on the Costa Tropical. The Spanish mostly go there so it is not overrun by tourists. The town has a lot of history as it was founded by the Phoenicians who called it Sexi, and it has also been occupied by the Romans, Visigoths, Muslims and Christians. The bay is lovely and the views from the cliff tops are breath-taking." Trevor could see from her eyes that she was picturing the town as she spoke. He was glad to see this as it gave her something to hang on to as they prepared for this rocky journey. "What about you Nick, how do you feel about that?" "I agree. It is a beautiful place and it's about an hour and a half from the ski resorts in Granada, so you can have the best of both worlds." "Sounds like a really nice place, I will have to check it out." Trevor decided that he needed them to now get their thoughts back on the business. "Would your goal of having an income of two hundred and fifty thousand a year allow you to go and live in Spain?" "Yes, it would." There was no hesitation in Nick's response. "Ok, so how are you going to achieve your goals?" Nick and Amanda glanced at each other before Nick answered, "I guess we have to carry on investing and building our portfolio." Trevor smiled. "Now that you have made that decision, you will have to commit to it." "Where do we start?" "Well, I have no doubt that there are some very clever people who are going to be in the same predicament as you, and they will be looking at the best ways to mitigate some of the problems so there may be some avenues to explore at a later stage. However, let's be clear. It is unlikely that the government will do a U-turn on their proposal so all that we can do is work on the areas that we can influence and with what is available to us." "How do we start?" "You have already started Nick. All the things you have been learning about and doing such as removing waste from your system, standard work, continuous improvement etc. is helping you to streamline your business and making you more effective and efficient. These are the areas we can influence. Then, we can look at what is available to you that you can leverage such as grants for refurbishments etc. You can turn your business into a limited company and use the company to buy your properties as it is advantageous doing it this way. Afterwards, look at what you can claim back on tax; for instance, your home office, depreciation of your printer, if you have shirts or T-shirts with your logo that's classed as work wear as it is company issued, you can claim back laundry and no doubt there are other things that you can claim that your financial advisor can tell you about. You need to do your research and leave no stone unturned. Remember to keep an eye on social media and use it as leverage as there will be other investors doing the same thing and telling everyone what they have found, and you must do the same as getting through this is all about teamwork." Amanda got up from her chair and faced Trevor. "Can I give you a hug please?" Trevor smiled as he got up to receive his hug "Thank you," Amanda whispered in his ear.

When Amanda left the room to go and make them a drink, Nick thanked Trevor as he was just glad to see Amanda happy once again, and he felt that a light had been shone down a dark tunnel. It wasn't long before Amanda appeared with a tray full of drinks and they took a moment to reflect as they sipped on their drinks. "Right guys. I'm going to show you a new way of thinking about your accounts called throughput accounting. This is taken from a continuous improvement method called the theory of constraints or TOC for short. As you will see, it is a simple but powerful tool because we can look at how to increase your throughput, which in your case is building up your housing stock to obtain a larger portfolio. "What did you call it again?" Amanda asked. "Throughput accounting or TA for short. It was developed by a very clever physicist called Eliyahu Goldratt and it made its debut in the nineteen eighties. It was primarily developed to give managers up to date information with less calculations than the traditional cost accounting methods." "I have never heard of it, and it certainly wasn't mentioned during my book keeping course." Nick nodded in agreement with Amanda, as he too had not come across throughput accounting. "I'm not surprised Amanda. It's not that popular because the traditional accountant still rules the roost. Let me ask you a question. Did they ever mention as part of the discussion in your class that the way to save money is to cut operating expenses ?" Amanda thought for a minute. "Yes, they did. We had a case study of a manufacturing company and we had to look at ways of saving money, so we cut operating expenses first as much as possible and then looked at reducing the inventory. This would have saved the company a large amount of money." Amanda was pleased that she had remembered this, as it was her first assignment and she had scored well in it. "I can see where you are going with this. We should apply the same technique to our business; that way we can make some good savings and we will end up with more profit." "Actually, no Amanda, we are not going to use the traditional method that you have described as it is completely wrong." Amanda was puzzled. "How can it be wrong, if this is the method that is used worldwide?" "Just because it is used by many doesn't mean that it is correct. If we go back in history, the world believed that the earth was flat and that if you sailed far enough, you would go over the edge. A few people risked their lives to disprove that theory and we all know that they were right, and the rest of the world was wrong. Throughput accounting falls into that category as you will see when I explain it to you." Nick and Amanda were now intrigued and wanted to know more. Trevor asked for a whiteboard. Nick went off to his office to get one. A minute later, the whiteboard was set up in the living room. Trevor took a whiteboard pen and began to draw.

"Throughput is all the money that is coming in. It is generated by your property deals, either through rent and initially, the value of the property or sale of property. Investment is all of your money that is tied up in the properties that you intend to rent or sell but at this moment in time do not have customers, and by customers, I mean either a tenant or a buyer. Finally, operating expenses is the money that is going out in terms of things such as utilities, consumable supplies, labour etc." "So, what you are saying is that, we need to look at the throughput rather than looking at operating expenses?" Yes Nick. A large number of organisations say that they are in business to make money, yet they spend an awful lot of their time cutting costs. This is divergent thinking as it takes the organisation in a different direction and results in different results. If the goal of an organisation is to save money, then the best way they can achieve this is simply by going out of business. If the real goal is to make money, then the organisation needs to increase throughput throughout the system. By all means, you can reduce investment and operating expenses so long as it does not affect throughput." Amanda's mind was a whirl with questions. "I get what you are saying, but how do you measure things like return on investments, net profit, etc.?" "Let me write it down for you so that you can see." Once again, Trevor picked the whiteboard pen and began to write.

Net Profit (NP) = Throughput (T) minus Operating Expense (OE) or

NP = T – OE

Return On Investment (ROI) = Net Profit (NP) divided by Investment (I) or

ROI = NP/I

Productivity (P) = Throughput (T) divided by Operating Expense (OE) or

P = T/OE

Inventory Turns (IT) = Throughput (T) divided by Inventory Value (IV) or

IT = T/I

"Net Profit can be increased by either increasing the throughput or decreasing the operating expenses. Productivity is expressed as a ratio rather than the difference between throughput and operating expenses. Return on Investment can be increased through increasing net profit or decreasing investment required to create that amount of profit. Investment turns is the amount of throughput created per unit of investment. With these four simple formulas, you can see how you are doing as a business on a daily, weekly or monthly basis and adjust your business accordingly." Amanda had an epiphany moment. "I get it! Cost accounting is all about the actions you take to save money and throughput accounting is all about the action you take to make money." Amanda had a huge smile on her face when Trevor agreed with her. "You are spot on Amanda. Therefore, your action is to increase the number of properties that you either rent or sell which is your throughput, whilst at the same time reducing your operating expense by removing waste from your system, working with suppliers to reduce costs, obtaining grants and claiming money back on tax, etc." "What about investment? Is there anything we can do about that?" Nick asked. Trevor smiled. "You can reduce your investment by finding a joint venture partner or raising angel finance so that you can do a lot more deals and you're not reliant on the bank for loans and buy-to-let mortgages. You can also improve investment by selling and/or refurbishing your properties quickly."

"Duh, of course! I think I have just had a brain fade." They all good-humouredly laughed with Nick, and Trevor was delighted, as the energy in the room had changed from negativity to a positively one.

"Now we are going to get serious about your business, by adding structure to it, as this will allow you to scale your business up." "But there are only two of us, so is there any point?" Nick asked. "There may only be two of you at this moment in time but as we have just discussed, you are going to increase your throughput, and to increase your throughput, you will have to start expanding. If we leave things as they are, when the time comes, you will be scrambling about on the back foot and it will take time to catch up, which will lead to lost opportunities." "Ok, what do we start with?" Amanda asked with anticipation. "We should start by defining your organisation's objectives." "We are not an organisation; we are a small business," Nick objected. "Nick, you need to change your thinking. If you have a small business mentality, you will always be small, and you will never grow, which means you will always be dealing with pennies rather than pounds." Nick took a deep breath. "Ok, I hear what you're saying, so how do we choose our objectives?" "Well, you have told me what your goals are, so how do we meet those goals?" "I guess right now I'm not sure." "Ok, let's start with your mission statement as this will tell us what your company is all about." "Hmm, that is a difficult one as we have never thought about it." Amanda agreed with Nick. "Come up with some words and we will see what we can put together." Nick and Amanda did as they were asked whilst Trevor wrote them down. It was not long before they had a list of words and Nick and Amanda found it difficult to come up with more.

Growth	Exceed	Serve
Quality	Generate	Revolutionise
Home	Implement	Resolve
Care	Lead	Improve
Focus	Increase	Facilitate
Deliver	Promote	Exist
Establish	Integrate	Excite
Dominate	Transform	Challenge
Create	Accelerate	Connect

"What words can we use from your list to come up with a mission statement?" They stared at the list and tried to compose a mission statement in their heads. "How about 'NAC properties challenge the norm by providing quality homes because we care about and focus on our tenants'." "That's not bad Amanda. What about you Nick, can you do any better?" Nick concentrated and stared at the list for a few minutes before answering. "NAC properties will dominate the market by exceeding the quality expected by our tenants because we transform a house into a home." "Good effort Nick. Can we do better?" "This is harder than I thought." "Yes it is Amanda, and some companies never get it right or don't live up to their mission statements. That's why it is important to spend some time on it." "I think that we are trying too hard. I'm going to make us a drink." Amanda got up and went to the kitchen. Nick kept on staring at the words and composing a mission statement in his mind. Amanda appeared with a tray full of coffee mugs and passed them around. They relaxed as they sipped on their drinks. "Remember, these words are just here to help you. If you can come up with others, that's fine." "NAC properties are a caring company that focuses on its tenants by adding value and quality to their properties and transforming them from houses to homes." "That's good Amanda. Nick, are you happy with Amanda's suggestion?" Nick nodded enthusiastically. "I think it is bang on, I can't think of anything better." "Now that you have told me what your mission statement is, you can come up with objectives that meet your mission statement." "Is there a method we can use to come up with objectives that we could use?" asked Nick. "Look at your mission statement and tell me what your key words are." "Focus, value, quality, transform, homes." "Ok, let's take your first word; how are you going to focus on your tenants?" "By understanding their needs through talking to them." "So, what you are saying Amanda is that you're going to be customer centric?" "Yes, that way, we will get to know our tenants." "Good. Now, how will you measure that?" Nick and Amanda thought hard about it and suddenly, it dawned on Nick. "We can measure it through questionnaires, customer complaints and voids." "Good. Now, what is your objective for value?" "We can add value to our properties and measure that by looking at the difference between the bought value and the done-up value." "Very good Nick. Now you're thinking." Nick almost beamed from Trevor's unexpected praise. Amanda saw it and made them all smile when she said, "that was beginners' luck." "Next word." The quality of the materials and workmanship will be high. We can measure this not only through the done-up value but also by using tenant questionnaires and monitoring supplier quality." "Very good Amanda. You now have two words left: transform and homes." "I would like to transform ourselves from a small home-based business to a larger business." "Ok Nick. So how are you going to do that?" "First of all, by growing our portfolio, and then by becoming well known for the quality of our properties." "So, what you're saying is that, you will transform the business through expansion and branding and you will measure it through the amount of conversion of investment into properties with cash flow?" "Yes, that's exactly what I want to do." Trevor turned to Amanda and asked, "do you agree with Nick?" "It sounds like hard work, but as you said earlier, we need to start thinking bigger." "Now you're on your last word." "Tenants staying long term and we can measure it by the number of voids that we have." "Looks like we are done, thanks to Amanda." Nick smiled. "Not quite. Sum it up so we can obtain your objectives." Nick cleared his throat, but Amanda beat him to it. "Customer first, Add Value, work with our suppliers, become big enough to cope but small enough to care." "Nicely summed up Amanda. You now have a mission statement and objectives that you can measure, so now you have direction. In effect, this is your compass as it will try and point you to your true North." Nick and Amanda looked pleased with themselves; they had come a long way since last night when they were feeling so despondent. It had been a long hard morning; they decided to break for lunch.

After about an hour, they got back to work. "What's next?" asked Nick eagerly. "Now, you need to look at your marketing strategy and determine what you need to do to meet your objectives." Trevor waited for his words to sink in. "Now I'm totally out of my depth. I know nothing about marketing." Amanda agreed with Nick. "Me neither and I wouldn't know where to start." "Actually, you have been doing some marketing already." Nick and Amanda shook their heads, whilst Trevor looked at them amused at their denial. "No, we haven't. I told you, we know nothing about marketing." Nick spoke for both of them. "Tell me what you are doing when you go to networking events?" "We are building relationships." "Why are you building relationships?" Amanda spoke up. "To help each other by swapping ideas." "So, are you not offering your services?" "I suppose we are in a way," Nick agreed reluctantly. "So, you become the go to person for advice when it comes to specialised topics?" "I guess so; I don't get your point." "Why do they come to see you?" "Because, like you said, I have knowledge on certain topics." Nick was puzzled by the questioning. "Hun, don't you see, Trevor is saying that you are known because of your own brand, which is a form of marketing." Nick looked across at Trevor for confirmation, who in turn nodded in agreement with Amanda. "I think I am beginning to see where you are coming from. By networking and giving out business cards, we are actually marketing our personal brand." "Yes, that is exactly what you are doing. So, as you can see, you are already involved in marketing. Now we need to take it a step higher by building your portfolio" "Now that I think about it, we have tried to market and build our portfolio by using a leaflet drop, but it wasn't very successful." "How many other businesses were you competing with?" "At least three that we know of." "No Hun, there were four and rumours of another two." Nick was thoughtful for a minute, "yes, you are right, it was four." "So, what differentiated you from the others?" Trevor asked. Nick and Amanda looked at each other, each hoping that the other would remember something that made their leaflets stand out from the others. Nick reluctantly turned to Trevor. "I guess there was no real difference between us all." Amanda agreed, "they were all written on yellow paper with all of the usual wording. I guess it's because we all learnt about it in the same way and we more or less copied each other." "Do you have one of your leaflets knocking about that I could see?" Amanda got up. "I think there may be one or two in my folder in the office. If not, I can print one. Whilst I'm doing that, Nick be a sweetheart and put the kettle on."

Ten minutes later, they were sipping their drinks whilst Trevor was reading through the leaflet that Amanda had printed out. "This is not very inspiring, and it highlights a lot of negativity that people do not want to be reminded of. They already know that they are going to sell their property, so your job is to show them how easy the process can be for them."

We Buy House

- Debt
- Illness
- Redundancy
- Repossessions
- Relocations
- Divorce
- Selling Problems
- Negative Equity
- Bereavement

We Can Help!

- ✓ Confidential
- ✓ Free Consultation
- ✓ No Chain
- ✓ No Legal Fees
- ✓ No Obligations

Text or Call Amanda: 079874562128

"How do we do that? How can we be different?" asked Amanda. Trevor thought about it for a moment. "How about if you had a leaflet with the mapped-out process for estate agents and another map that shows what you can offer?" With that, Trevor took the whiteboard marker pen and began to draw a map. He then cut out the picture from Amanda's leaflet.

We Buy Houses

How we are different from an Estate Agent

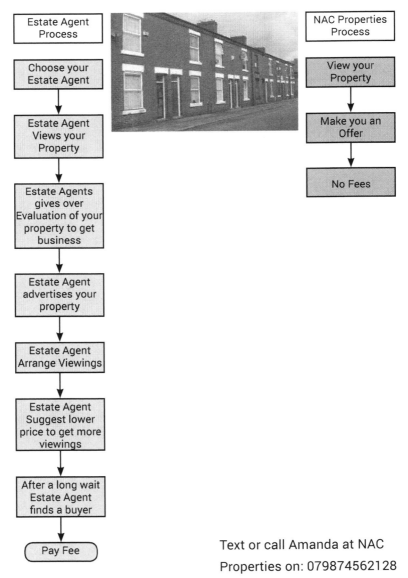

Estate Agent Process		NAC Properties Process
Choose your Estate Agent		View your Property
↓		↓
Estate Agent Views your Property		Make you an Offer
↓		↓
Estate Agents gives over Evaluation of your property to get business		No Fees
↓		
Estate Agent advertises your property		
↓		
Estate Agent Arrange Viewings		
↓		
Estate Agent Suggest lower price to get more viewings		
↓		
After a long wait Estate Agent finds a buyer		
↓		
Pay Fee		

Text or call Amanda at NAC Properties on: 079874562128

"Wow, that really stands out." Amanda agreed with Nick. "The map makes all the difference." "Yes, it does, by showing all of the steps you are showing your potential sellers two ways to sell, with one its long term whilst the other is very quick. Therefore, seeing this through the eyes of a seller who needed to sell quickly they would naturally take the quickest option, so in effect with this leaflet you are teaching your seller to see." "This should really motivate them, but won't the agents get upset?" Amanda inquired. "Interesting question Amanda, but let me ask you one, why did you do the leaflet drop in the first place? "I guess it was because everyone else was doing it and we heard that they had good results, but when we tried we didn't receive any calls and so we thought it best just to build relationships with the agents." "You probably didn't get any results because all of you were going for the same types of properties because that is what you were taught, which is why you need to differentiate yourself from everyone else. So, to answer your question, no Amanda, the agents will be fine with it, as they know that the odds are stacked in their favour. You see most people will tell you that they don't like change so the concept that we are presenting will not be taken up by everyone, as they will opt for the more traditional route as they are comfortable with it as they understand it. However, you only need one person to take you up and you're on your way. So, to do this properly you need what the RAF call a surgical strike." Nick was intrigued, "What do you mean?" "When the RAF wants to take out a particular target, they make sure that is what they hit and nothing else. You need to do the same by picking a street that you are really interested in and you target your leaflets just in that street, because;

my guess is that in the past you have gone for a shotgun approach and hit lots of streets over a wide area, so you have wasted a lot of time and money doing this. By being more clinical you are taking waste out of your system and you are concentrating in an area that you really want." "Yes, you are right, we did have a shotgun approach as we wanted to cover a wide area just hoping that we would get a response. I can see that your approach makes more sense, and we could, on average. do a street in about fifteen minutes rather than hours for an area. So, as you say we would be freeing up our time and we wouldn't need so many leaflets." "You could use the just in time method. To obtain your leaflets that way you don't have leaflets hanging about the house, and because you will know how many houses there are in the street that you are interested in, you can order or print the exact number of leaflets that you require, so you will also save money." "That works for me; I wish we had known how to do this a couple of years ago when we first started " Nick said. "Don't beat yourself up Nick, it's a case of you don't know what you don't know." "I guess, but I get the feeling that I should have known." "Sometimes you are too close to your business because you are working in it rather than on it, so you don't see these things. You need to learn to take a step back and have an overview of your business without getting emotional about it and become a problem solver." "I can see that now, it just needed to be pointed out to me." "You're not the only one Hun, remember this is my business too and I didn't look at the bigger picture either." "You're right, we need to move on and not dwell on the past." Trevor was pleased to hear Nick's response especially considering how the day had started with the pair of them being so negative.

"As you both have mentioned the bigger picture; we are now going to take a look at your business from that point of view. We are going to start with your organisation chart " Amanda looked confused. "In case you haven't noticed, there are only two of us." Trevor smiled; this is something that he had heard often when helping small and medium size businesses. "I had noticed; however, we are going to be looking at the different job roles that you do. I take it that you are both directors of your company." "We are joint owners, if that's what you mean." Trevor went on, "As you are going to be growing your company and maybe become a limited company, so if it is alright with you Amanda, we will use the term directors as I need you to start to think about the direction you want to take the company." Amanda nodded in assent and waited to hear what Trevor would say. "Although you are both directors, who is the CEO?" Nick and Amanda looked at each other and Nick answered, "I would say that is me." "Who is the financial director?" Nick reluctantly answered again, "I guess that is also me." Trevor was not surprised. "Who is the operations manager?" Amanda looked up "That's me." "Ok, so who is the logistics manager?" "That is also me" Amanda answered. "Right, who is the secretary/administrator?" "That's me again," Trevor acknowledged Amanda. "Ok, now I am going to make this visual for you." With that, Trevor picked up a whiteboard marker and began to draw.

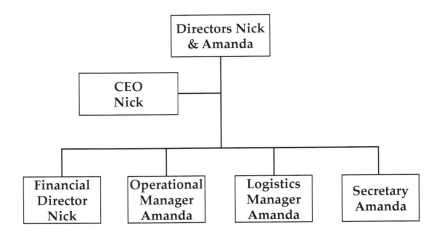

"What is that telling you?" asked Trevor pointing at the board. "That we have multi-roles" replied Nick. "So, in reality what you are saying is that you are multi-tasking." Both Nick and Amanda agreed with Trevor, "I'm a woman so multi-tasking comes natural to me" Amanda quipped. Trevor smiled "Sorry to burst your bubble but multi-tasking is not good for running your business, or in fact your life, as things don't get done quickly and more often than not they lead to mistakes." "I disagree; I have to multi-task as it is the only way I can get my work done." "Ok Amanda, the only way I am going to convince you is to show you." So once again, Trevor picked up the marker pen and began to draw.

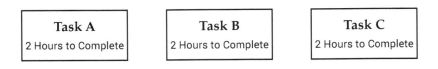

"Here are three tasks that need to be completed and we are going to say for the purpose of this exercise that it takes two hours to complete each task. Because of the perceived idea that multi-tasking is a good way of being able to complete these tasks we are going to apply it. So, we will spend an hour on each task."

Task A	**Task B**	**Task C**
1 Hour spent on task	1 Hour spent on task	1 Hour spent on task

"So, we have now spent a total of three hours and we haven't yet completed a task. We now go back to task A and we finish it. It has taken a total of four hours to complete task A whereas if you had completed task A before moving on to task B it would have only taken you two hours, plus you will have to remember what you were doing as your train of thought would have been lost due to moving between jobs, so your increasing the chances of mistakes happening." Amanda stared at the diagram and played over in her mind what Trevor had said and she came to the reluctant conclusion that he was right, and she was wrong. "You have made your point; I can't disagree with you." Nick nodded in agreement "It is no wonder we waste a lot of time trying to get things done." "What we need to do is to try and free up some of your time, so consider hiring someone on a part time basis to do your administration work." "Do you mean a virtual assistant?" Nick asked. "No, a virtual assistant is fine for some work after you have trained them in what you need doing, but often these assistances are in different time zones and if you need something done now then it could be difficult." Nick was curious, "Where would you use a virtual assistant then?" "In your business I would use them to do the research to find properties and get them to pass them on to you, as that would free up your time scrolling through pages of properties, or to maintain your social media presence to help you with your brand. However, for the day-to-day administration, I would have a person that would come to your office and help you with the paperwork and if they are efficient and trustworthy then you could start to train them to do other things in your business. "Won't that cost us quite a bit of money, whereas at the moment it doesn't cost us anything?" Nick persisted. "You are missing the point Nick, you are looking at a minor cost compared to the bigger picture, and you need to think of it as a short-term loss for a long-term gain." "Trevor is right Hun, if you think about it we have been penny pinching in the past and although it has got us where we are now, we have been hitting a brick wall every time we have tried to expand." Before Nick could protest, Amanda moved the direction of the conversation on "Where would be the best place to find someone to hire?" Trevor decided that he needed to appease Nick whilst answering Amanda "You could see if a local college or university have people that are looking to gain some work experience, so not only would it keep your costs down, but you would also help that person get a job in the future as they can use it on their CV." This appealed to Nick just as Trevor thought it would, "That is a great idea, could we use it for anything else?" "I was going to suggest that the next job that you hire for is book keeping, as you need to know your numbers on a regular basis such as your profit and loss, how much is spent on expenses, and how much cash you have available to you. This is something that you need to know on a weekly basis in conjunction with throughput accounting so that you can see where you are. The book keeper will also make things easier for your accountant hence, it will reduce the time they have to spend on your books and give you advice quickly when you need it." "Thinking about it, it would free us up to start working on our business and not in our business." Trevor and Amanda smiled; it looks like Nick was at last starting to become a convert.

"I need you both to pull it all together now by creating a top-level manual that describes your business." Nick was apprehensive, "That sounds daunting." "What should it include?" Amanda asked. "Don't look so worried it is not as bad as you think, it just needs a bit of thought and an understanding of your business. The manual needs to be a live document, in that you review it regularly and make changes as your business evolves. As far as contents are concerned I want you to keep it simple so work on these headings." Trevor picked up the marker pen and began to write on the whiteboard.

1.   Scope – A brief summary of the manual (one or two lines)

2.   Purpose – Defines the manual and how it will meet company and customer requirements (one or two lines)

3.   Mission Statement

4.   Vision Statement

5.   Objectives

6.   Introduction

7. Documentation Requirements

    ↳ Procedures   ↳ Document Control   ↳ Record Control

8. Monitoring and Measuring

    ↳ KPI's (Key Performance Indicators)   ↳ Customer Satisfaction ↳ Audits/Questionnaires

9. Management Review

    ↳ A full review of the business   ↳ Inputs into the business ↳ Outputs ↳ Frequency of Reviews

10. Human Resources

    ↳ Competence   ↳ Awareness   ↳ Training

11. Client related Processes

    ↳Contracts ↳Questionnaires ↳Joint Venture Requirements ↳ Legal Requirements

12. Client Communication

    ↳ Issues   ↳ Records

13. Purchasing Information

    ↳ Evaluation of Suppliers   ↳ Performance Criteria   ↳ Procurement Records ↳ Verification of Purchased Products

14. Improvements

    ↳ Continuous Improvement   ↳ Corrective Actions   ↳ Preventive Actions

"That looks like a long list," Nick observed. "Not really, when you start to break it down each of these headings will only have a few paragraphs, I have given you suggestions of what to consider within the headings, however what is important is the content not the quantity. Remember, this is a guideline you may want to add or subtract from it. However, I would rather at this stage that you add and not subtract. By thinking about it and writing it down you are more likely to commit to it, and as your business grows you can hand the manual over to your employee to read so that they have a good understanding about your organisation without you having to explain everything. So in effect, you are using a process to start their training. Also, the manual is a way of showing a possible investor for a joint venture that you have knowledge and control of your business, and should you decide to sell your business in the future, you will obtain a higher price as you will have a systemised business with processes in place so that it can run independently from you, which makes it very attractive to a buyer." Nick pondered over what Trevor had said. "Interesting; I can see where you're coming from and it makes a lot of sense." "I agree with Nick, and from what you and Brian have shown us I can see how our business will start to get better and we can go from strength to strength. I for one, certainly, am in a better place than I was in these last couple of days and I feel rejuvenated and want to make our business really successful." "I am glad to hear it; any business can be created or improved so long as you have clear objectives, a strategy in place to reach those objectives and tactics that will help you achieve your strategy. You know what your objectives are, your strategy is to systemise your business, drive out waste, work with your suppliers and work on your business and not in your business and marketing is one of your tactics, so you have a starting point to launch a successful business." Time had gone quickly as they realised it was early evening, so Trevor bid Nick and Amanda farewell and told them that he would inform Brian of the day's topics and activities, as he would be unavailable for a few days, but they had enough to go on to keep them busy until Brian was available to help them with the next stage.

Chapter Seven

Trevor decided to ring Brian when he got home, after the third ring Brian answered. "Hello Trevor, how did it go with Nick and Amanda?" "It started off with them being quite negative especially Amanda, but as the day progressed they became quite positive and by the end of the day they were thinking more about their business and working on it instead of in it, so they have turned a corner." "That is good news, I was quite worried about Amanda, as Nick said it seemed to affect her more, which is surprising really as she seemed the more positive of the two." "She is more positive and importantly more passionate, and it was because she feels that way that she takes things personally, so you need to remind them to work on their business by using their objectives, strategy and tactics and don't let them stray away from it." I will make sure that they stay on track, especially when we go to the refurbishment and loft conversion stage, as no doubt Nick will want to skimp and save as we have yet to really break this habit." "Make sure that they are there every day of the build and get them to do a Gemba walk along with the other activities we have planned." "No problem I will be on it." "Thank you Brian and I will call in to your office next week when you're back and we can do some more work on your business." "Look forward to it, and we can go to lunch for a catch up." "I will hold you to it, and you are paying." Brian was still smiling when they said their goodbyes and Trevor hung up.

Nick and Amanda decided to allocate two hours of their time every day to work on their manual. At first, they had struggled to decide what to put under each of the headings and disagreements were inevitable but slowly their manual began to come together. It was during one of these sessions that Nick suddenly had a thought; he had remembered a lecture in his college days when he and Trevor were engineering apprentices about a quality standard that gave guidance on quality systems that could help them with the manual. Nick racked his brain, but he could not remember what the standard was called, after all it was a long while back and at the age of seventeen and still wet behind the ears he did not pay it much attention, so he did an internet search and it wasn't long before he found what he was looking for, ISO 90001. Nick checked the price to buy it and was taken back. *Wow! that is expensive for a small document,* he thought. Therefore, he began an online check of his local library to see if they had a copy and as luck would have it they did, but it was reference only so he would have to make notes whilst he was there. Nick told Amanda about it and they decided that there was no time like the present, so they set off to library.

Nick approached the help desk and asked the librarian for the standard he was looking for, he was given a copy and he and Amanda sat at one of the many empty tables took out their note books and with eager anticipation began to read through the standard. They could see that the headings that were given to them by Trevor were also in the standard. However, there was a whole lot more and it gave them food for thought about risk-based thinking when it came to planning and taking action to address risks and opportunities. Although the standard was only twenty-nine pages long, it was packed full of information that was helpful in laying out a management system that they could apply to their business. Although it only took them a short time to read through it, it took a lot longer to write notes as they discussed the usefulness of each section and how it applied to their business. As Nick was finishing off reading his notes, Amanda decided to have a wander around the library. She went over to the section that dealt with business and manufacturing and browsed a few books, she was scanning a few titles to see if anything peaked her interest, when she saw a title that she thought was out of place for the section, it was called Learning to See. Amanda was curious, so she picked it up, started flicking through it, and immediately stopped. Taking the book, she went back to Nick. "Guess what I have found." "Go on." "A book on mapping." She showed Nick the book and they both started to look through it. "This is what Trevor and Brian have been trying to show us and here it is laid out in an easy to read way. Although this is for manufacturing, I can see how it can be applied to anything, it just makes sense and reinforces what we were taught." "I agree Hun, and I am so glad that you asked Trevor to help us out. By the way, you have never explained why you asked him." "I can't really explain it, I had just received a call telling me we had a void, and Trevor just mentioned in a casual way a couple of things that made sense, and I had this strange feeling and a little voice in my head just said to ask for help, so I just came out with it and asked him." "Sometimes you just have to go with your gut feeling, as the old saying goes, when you need a teacher one will show up, and we have got two of them." Before they left the library Amanda wanted to see if they had some books that would help with their mind-set, so she browsed the shelves in the self-help section and found two that she liked the look of as they were of a practical nature and so seemed right for her, they were called Step Up and F.O.C.U.S and 4@13@7 System and as chance would have it they were by the same author. They checked the books out and they agreed that they would have to come to the library more often as they had not been in such a long while and here was a source of untapped information from other industries that could be applied to their own business which would make them unique in their field and therefore stand out from the rest of the crowd.

A few days later Amanda got emails from two of the three architects that she had sent the enquiry forms to, she downloaded and printed off the completed forms and then began to read through them. One of the architects was unavailable for nine months and the other was even longer, however he gave Amanda details of another architect who had just finished five major developments and was winding down as he was considering retirement but may be persuaded to do a few small jobs before he did. Amanda quickly sent off the enquiry form along with an explanation of how she had been given his contact details by his friend and that she would be grateful if he could take on a small project so that she could also learn from his experience. An hour later Amanda received an email from the architect with the completed form and telling her that he would be available within two weeks, he also told her that he would be bringing along his son who would be taking over the business. Although he had been teaching him, he wanted him to go solo on this project whilst he would be observing him to ensure that he did everything correct and of course would take full responsibility for the project. Amanda emailed him back and agreed that he could start and let him use the opportunity for his son to come up with the plans. Amanda was so excited and couldn't wait to tell Nick that she had found an architect. "Amanda what have you done?" Nick's response to her news was not something that she had expected. "I have found an architect who can start straight away, what's wrong with that?" "We are supposed to get three estimates and then narrow it down, you have just jumped straight in without even knowing anything about this guy." Amanda took a deep breath, she knew that Nick was right "I'm sorry Hun, I guess I was so disappointed with the length of time before we go an architect and when this one said he was available within two weeks I just thought I had better snap him up before someone else did." Nick could understand where Amanda was coming from, but he needed to drive a point home "I understand, however if this guy produces a design or plan that is not what we are looking for then not only would it set us back in time, it would also cost us money, and as a business we cannot afford to lose either." Amanda was feeling a little angry with herself for not thinking things through, "Do you want me to get back to him and cancel?" Nick thought about it for a few moments, "Before we decide to cancel, let's do a due diligence and find out about his work, and talk to some of his clients." Amanda was relieved that

Nick had come up with a partial solution, which could show that the architect is right for them. "I'll do it now." Amanda quickly went off to the office to start her search on the internet to learn all about her architect.

A few hours later Amanda appeared and showed Nick the information that she had printed off, "It appears that this architect is just what we are looking for. He designs residential housing both for developers and private owners." Nick looked through the print outs that Amanda had handed over to him, after ten minutes of reading he looked up, "It appears that you have struck lucky, however I want you to contact him and ask him if we can see some of his projects and talk to the owners." Amanda felt relieved that Nick had so far approved her architect, if he gave the thumbs up after seeing his work that would be the icing on the cake, and she felt she had just learnt a valuable lesson in the art of being patient. "Ok I will contact him now and make the arrangements." Amanda now felt and sounded more confident as she went off to the office, Nick watched her go and was amazed at the change in her.

"I have had a reply from our architect Max McNeill, he is more than happy for us to look at his work and to talk to his customers, he has given me a list of all of his latest projects, so we just need to pick some to view and he will try to arrange with the owners for us to have a viewing." Nick was pleased as this was turning out to be quite positive. "Ok, seeing as you have done all of the work, you can pick the ones for us to view." Amanda scanned down the list and decided on three in different areas that way she could have a good cross section of the projects. She returned to the office to make the arrangements. Twenty minutes later, Amanda came running into the living room, "Nick we have got to go now for a viewing." "Whoa! what do you mean we have to go now, explain yourself?" "The owners of one of the houses that we wanted to see are about to go on holiday for three weeks, they only have this afternoon available for us to view and we have to get over to Ansty near Coventry. So, grab your coat and let's get going." Nick galvanised himself into action and grabbed his coat and car keys and followed Amanda out to his car. It was not long before they were on the M6 motorway heading for junction 2. They turned off junction 2, joined the B4065, and drove on into Ansty. They found the address they were looking for, the house looked like the rest in the street, brick built with white façade. They got out of the car and went and knocked at the door. A minute later, the door opened and a woman of about forty, five feet five, with blond hair and blue eyes greeted them. "You must be Amanda and Nick." "Yes, we are, and you are Sharon I presume" replied Amanda. Sharon shook hands with them, "Do come in." With that, she let them through and into the house. The house was quite modern and contemporary inside with wide-open plan kitchen/diner and very light and airy. Sharon showed them around and pointed out all of the features, and then she showed them some before photographs, then the plans and photographs of the build stages. "Do you mind if I take some photographs?" Amanda asked. "Please do," Sharon was amused with Amanda's enthusiasm. Whilst Amanda was taking photographs, Nick continued to review the document with Sharon. "So how did you find Max as an architect?" Nick asked. "He was very good, we told him what our budget was and what we wanted to achieve, he then produced a number of sketches to give us an idea what was possible. Once we decided what we wanted he produced the plans, the scheme of works and all of the relevant paperwork and the builders just got on with it. Max kept an eye on it throughout the build, but to be honest the detail that he provided was so good that the builders rarely had to consult with him." "So, you would recommend him then?" "Absolutely, in fact I have recommended him to my aunt only yesterday as she wants to do a barn conversion." Nick and Amanda glanced at each other and perceptively nodded, they had both liked what they had seen and heard. An hour and a half later and after they had thanked Sharon for showing them around the house and answering their questions, they were in the car on their way home. "What do you think?" Amanda asked. "It looks like we are onto a winner; if the other houses and owners are like this one then we will be offering him the job." Over the next several days, they managed to visit the properties that were on Amanda's list and came away feeling very positive as each homeowner praised the architect and had nothing negative to say about him.

Brian was greeted enthusiastically by Amanda when he arrived for their meeting, she could not wait to tell him the news about the architect. As soon as he was sat down in the living room, Amanda and Nick told him about the architect and how they had visited the properties that he had designed and were impressed with his work. They showed him the documents from their due diligence and some photographs of the houses that they had visited. "It appears that although you went off track, it has in this instance paid off; just don't make a habit of it." "I won't, Nick gave me a hard time of it, so lesson learnt." "Well, at least we have a potential principle designer in place. Consequently, that will help with complying with the CDM twenty fifteen regulations." "What is that?" Nick asked. Brian regarded Nick for a second before asking the question "What is your business?" "Property investing of course, why do you ask?" "As a professional property investor should you not know about the regulations that can affect your business?" Nick became a bit flustered. "Well yes, I suppose that I should." "CDM twenty fifteen is one of those regulations that you should know about as it affects you every time you carry out a refurbishment." "We have never heard of it before now," Amanda added. "Ok, I think I had better explain. CDM stand for the Construction Design and Management which is a regulation that was brought out in twenty fifteen, hence CDM twenty fifteen. The regulation is about health and safety and how we apply it in the construction industry." Nick interrupted, "But ours is only a small build with just a loft conversion." "Nick, this regulation applies to any building except your own personal private resident, so this does affect you and your business." "But surely the builder will look after health and safety, after all his guys work for him so he is responsible for the site." "Sorry Nick, it doesn't work like that, the regulation is quite clear and lays out the duties of the client. I suggest that we download the regulations from the government website so that you can review it." Amanda volunteered to download and print off the documents. Whilst she was away, Nick asked Brian about the regulation, "How did you know about this regulation especially as you're not really a property guy?" "In my job, I work with different people and in different companies to manage and or advise on their projects, so I get to see and hear a lot. On one occasion, I was working with a client who is a property development company when this regulation came out. So, I had to understand it in case it delayed or changed the project. Health and safety has become important in the construction industry as at one point, there were lots of injuries and fatalities, so the government needed to do something about it. Over the years, the injuries and fatalities have been reduced significantly, but it is still not good enough. The CDM twenty fifteen regulations have been put in place for smaller builds to ensure that they too will comply with and understand what is required from a health and safety point of view. Amanda appeared with a set of documents each so that they review it. They looked through the lengthy document, which was quite comprehensive and took a little while to digest. "Wow this looks scary." Amanda observed. Nick looked worried, "I agree I don't know where to start." "It can be a bit daunting but don't let it faze you; it's just a learning curve for you." "A real steep one" Nick observed. "If we look at the regulation it tells you what your client duties are." They all turned to the relevant page and began to read the section that told them about their duties. "So, what does this mean in laymen terms?" asked Nick. "Basically, you need to appoint a principle designer, which is your architect, and your principle contractor which is Dave. You have already provided pre-construction information to Max with your form, so he has an idea of what you want to do. Dave has been to the property and knows what the job is all about; we just need to do this more formally.

You have to ensure that the people working on site have toilettes, washing facilities, drinking water, changing room and lockers and facilities for rest." "That is a lot of things that we need to supply and take care of," Amanda observed. "It is not as bad as you think as you have the property which already has some of these things in place that can be used. Anything else can be hired or constructed." "That will push the cost up!" Nick muttered. "What cost would you put on someone's health Nick?" Brian asked patiently. Nick knew it was wrong of him to even think about the cost when it came to health and regretted saying it. "I'm sorry I didn't mean it, I guess it was just being caught out by something I knew nothing about, and so I wasn't prepared for the extra work and costs that are required." "This is why you guys need to keep an eye out on all the regulations that can affect properties, I suggest that you have regular checks of the government website for changes in laws and the health and safety website for changes in regulations. Also, check out building and construction websites as these sometimes have whispers of a possible future regulation changes and they will have simplified versions on how to implement the changes." "Apart from the normal regulations for property we don't look any further. But you are right if we are in this business we should look deeper into anything that could have an impact on our business" Nick conceded. "The next thing that you have to ensure is that a risk assessment has been carried out for the work that potentially has inherited dangers." "I don't know what one looks like so how do I ensure that it is right?" Nick asked. "The best way to learn about it is if we construct one, and then you can use it as a guide or as a template for the future. In reality, your contractor should ensure that this is in place for all of the trades. Brian took his laptop out and set it up on the table and Nick and Amanda gathered around as Brian began to construct a risk assessment for them.

Risk Assessment				
Assessment No	Author	Approved By	Approved Date	Review Date
ABC 123	Nick Carrington	Brian Davies	9th June 2016	9th June 2017
Task:	Bricklayers			

Consequence						
Long Term Serious Injury / Illness or Fatality	5	5	10	15	20	25
Injury/Illness resulting in over 3-day absence	4	4	8	12	16	20
Injury/Illness resulting in up to 3-day absence	3	3	6	9	12	15
Minor injury requiring first aid	2	2	4	6	8	10
Scratch/Bruise	1	1	2	3	4	5
		1	2	3	4	5
		Almost Impossible	Unlikely	Possible	Likely	Almost Certain
		Likelihood				

Hazard Score		
Score	Action	Category
1 - 4	No Action is required; however, controls must be maintained	Acceptable

5 - 9	Make improvements within the agreed timescale	Low Risk
10 - 16	Urgent Action is required within the agreed timescale	High Risk
17 - 25	Stop Working and make improvements immediately	Unacceptable

Task Description

What are the Hazards?	Risk Score	Who may be harmed and How?	What are you currently doing?	What further action is required?	Action by whom?	Action by when?	Date done
Falling from height	15	Serious or fatal injuries may occur	1. Agree scaffolding requirements at contract stage, including appropriate load rating and provision of loading bays 2. Correct scaffold is provided and inspected. 3. Workers instructed not to interfere with or misuse scaffold. 4. Ladders in good condition, adequately secured (lashed) and placed on firm surface.	1. Scaffold requirements agreed, including loading bays and appropriate load rating. 2. Supervisor to speak regularly to site manager to arrange scaffold alterations and ensure that weekly inspections have been carried out.	NC	9/6/16	9/6/16

What are the Hazards?	Risk Score	Who may be harmed and How?	What are you currently doing?	What further action is required?	Action by whom?	Action by when?	Date done
Falling objects hitting head or body, including feet	15	Serious head and other injuries to workers, others on site and members of the public.	1. Brick guards in place 2. Waste material removed from scaffold and placed in the skip 3. Safety footwear and hard hats to be worn	Supervisor to monitor the use of Personal safety equipment	NC	9/6/16	9/6/16

147

What are the Hazards?	Risk Score	Who may be harmed and How?	What are you currently doing?	What further action is required?	Action by whom?	Action by when?	Date done
Manual Handling	16	All workers could suffer from back injury and long-term pain if regularly lifting/ carrying heavy or awkward objects.	1. Telehandler provided to transport bricks, cement etc. 2. Provide a lifting bay 3. Bricks to be covered by tarpaulin on site to prevent taking up water 4. Trolley to be used for moving bricks 5. Check at the tender stage for any blocks or lintels over 20kg and make arrangements	1. All workers instructed not to carry materials up by hand 2. Lintels over 20kg to be moved by telehandler 3. There are no blocks over 15kg so no action is required	NC	9/6/16	9/6/16

"This example is by no means complete but you get the idea of what it looks like." "How does this work?" asked Amanda. "You decide what the hazard is and then you look at the likelihood and the consequence and where the two points come together is the score that you apply. In this example, if we take the first hazard, which is falling from height, and we decide that the likelihood is possible, and the very real consequence could be a fatality then that gives us a score of fifteen, which tells us that it is a high risk, so we need to do something about it. So then, we look at what we are currently doing to see how we are mitigating the risk. If we believe there is a gap that needs to be addressed, we look at what further actions are required. A person who is responsible to ensure that it doesn't happen is then assigned the action, with the date that it was entered on the sheet and then finally the date that the action was completed is entered and then you move onto the next hazard etc." "So basically, it's like an action plan for hazards." "Yes, Amanda that is a good summary of what this is; the document may look different as each contractor will have their own version but so long as you can see it is an action plan then that's fine." "Do we have to make sure that they have these before they start work?" Nick asked. "Yes Nick, otherwise they are not allowed to start work. There will be an odd occasion that during the work something unforeseeable comes up that will need to be addressed. So then, you add it to the risk assessment, because the risk assessment is a live document until the work has been completed. Because they are live documents these documents need to be available to everyone on site, but they also need to be kept safe as this is also evidence that a risk assessment has been carried out." "What do we do with them after the job is finished?" asked Amanda. "The regulation is quite clear on that, as it tells you that you have to keep the health and safety files for the lifetime of the building as it may be used for other projects connected with the property such as extensions." "Now I get how it works, I don't feel intimidated by it," Nick commented. "I am glad that you said that, because you can also adapt the template for risk assessing your suppliers, such as letting agents." Amanda wanted to know more, "How do we do that?" she asked. "You simply substitute what you currently have in your health and safety risk assessment with things that you need to look at for a supplier. Therefore, you begin with the consequences in the table. Let me show you." Brian then began to make changes to the template as Nick and Amanda watched. "Then we change the likelihood followed by the hazard score to a risk score, then make changes to the actions." Brian made the changes as he spoke. "We then change the task description to supplier business risk." "That certainly does give us food for thought, we just need to play with it until we are comfortable with it" Nick observed. "That is like any tool or method that you use, the more that you employ it the more comfortable you will be with it until it becomes a habit."

Consequence		Possible	Occasionally	Likely	Very Likely	Almost Certain
	Continuous problems	5	5	10	15	20	25
	Poor customer service	4	4	8	12	16	20
	Caused a delay	3	3	6	9	12	15
	Occasional Problem	2	2	4	6	8	10
	An inconvenience	1	1	2	3	4	5
		1	2	3	4	5
		Possible	Occasionally	Likely	Very Likely	Almost Certain
		Likelihood				

Risk Score		
Score	**Action**	**Category**
1 - 4	No Action is required, however controls must be maintained	Acceptable
5 - 9	Periodic Monitoring	Low Risk
10 - 16	Continuous Monitoring until improvements are made	High Risk
17 - 25	Stop Working with them until improvements are made	Unacceptable

Supplier Business Risk

What are the Risks?	Risk Score	How does this affect the business?	What are you currently doing?	What further action is required?	Action by whom?	Action by when?	Date done
Wrong tenant	15	Unpaid rent Damage to the property	Reliant on the letting agent to screen tenant	1. Provide the agent with a model for them to follow to show what sort of tenant you are looking for 2. Ask the tenant to provide a guarantor	NC	9/6/16	9/6/16
Minor repairs not carried out	12	1. Property not maintained. 2. Tenant Leaves	Agent rings around for trades to make the repair	Employ a handyman on a retainer	NC	9/6/16	9/6/16

Nick nodded thoughtfully "When do we start using these?" he asked. "Prior to starting work. Have you made an appointment to meet with your architect Max?" "Not yet, we wanted to discuss it with you first and get your opinion, now that we have done that we can set up an appointment." Amanda replied. "I suggest that you set it up and also invite Dave and myself to the meeting, as I want us to work together as a team as this will iron out any problems that may come about." "When are you free Brian?" Amanda asked. Brian took out his phone and checked his calendar, "I am available at any time this month, as I am optional for the meetings that I do have penned in, so I don't have to be there." "Great, I will call Max and Dave now and see when they are available." With that, Amanda got up and went out to the office to make the calls. Nick decided to make them all a drink as time had moved on and they were not aware of it.

"Max and Dave are both available, all next week so we can get started on the design." Amanda had a huge grin as she made her announcement to Nick and Brian. "Someone's happy" Nick observed. "Yes, I can't wait to get started, as I want this to be a great project" Amanda replied. "Do you think that we can really get this done on time?" Nick asked Brian. Brian smiled "Yes Nick I do. What do you know about managing projects?" Nick thought about it, "Well, in my working days I used critical path and Gantt charts . So, I'm guessing that nothing has changed and that's what you'll be using." "Actually, no I'm not going to use the traditional project management tools, I am going to use a method called critical chain, as it is more efficient." Nick looked puzzled, "I have not come across that one before, what makes it so different?" he asked.

"Let me ask you a question first, how long will it take you to write your manual?" Nick thought about it before he replied. "Well we have done some research, so I would guess it should now only take a few days." "Are you are telling me it will take three days?" Brian asked to confirm Nick's answer. "Yes". "Ok Nick, I think that you can do it in less time, and here is why. Let me go through your thought process. First of all, your thoughts were that you could do the work in about a day and a half, but then you decided that you won't commit to that time scale just in case it was too tight. So, you added a time buffer by doubling your original figure as now you feel more comfortable in being able to deliver on time." Nick just stared at Brian in disbelief and then broke into a smile, "How did you know what I was thinking?" "Because you are no different from anyone else, nearly everybody who is given a task and is asked to give a time estimate will add a time buffer. A physicist called Goldratt had observed this and did some research on the subject." Amanda interrupted, "Sorry Brian, but is that the same Goldratt that created throughput accounting that Trevor told us about?" "Yes, it is; he also came up with a method called theory of constraints or TOC for short, which looks at trying to find the bottlenecks in your system so that they can be elevated so that you can improve your throughput." "You were telling us about time buffers," Nick was intrigued and wanted Brian to continue explaining it. "Yes of course, as I was saying Goldratt did some research and there were two things that stood out: student syndrome and Parkinson's Law." What is student syndrome?" Amanda asked. Nick turned to her, "When you were studying for an exam at school when did you decide to revise?"

Amanda thought back to her school days "The night before" she replied. "Why?" Amanda thought again before answering "At the time I had what I considered then more important things to do, like going out with my friends, going to the cinema, messing around, you know, girl things." "That in essence is student syndrome, you have plenty of time to do a bit of revision each day, but you leave it to the last minute and try to cram in as much revision as you can." Amanda smiled, "I understand completely what student syndrome is now." Brian smiled back "I am sure you do. Right the next one is Parkinson's Law, which states that the amount of work rises to fill the time available to complete it. In other words, people will complete then sit on the task and do other things or refine and improve the task until the due date and then hand it in." "So how were these observations applied to critical chain?" Nick asked. "Basically, Goldratt decided that the time buffer should be moved to the end of the project and work backward, so if you genuinely needed extra time you would draw on this time buffer. You also have feeder buffers along the chain, these are for longer tasks and they have their own mini time buffers, which are monitored. However, for it to work you would need people to be honest with their timescales and in some cases start the next task early without having to be told. You would also need to monitor the time buffer so that it does not run out before the end of the project." "Will that not be difficult to do? I mean people will not come clean and tell you exactly how long things will take, as it would be expected of them all of the time, it's almost like justifying their work" Nick asked. "You are right Nick, it is difficult and does mean a change of mind-set, so to help things along, we are going to get the work done by paying by the job and not by the hour. You see, if we pay by the hour then some people will eke it out so that they can earn more. However, by paying for the job, they will want to get on with it so that they can move onto the next job as quickly as possible. The next thing it to prevent multitasking. As we have already pointed out, this is not a good use of time. We also need to look at minimising resource contention, which is where the same piece of equipment is used to do different tasks and are required at the same time, so in effect it becomes multitasking for equipment."

"Can we go back to the time buffer please, as I am not sure that I really understood it from your description" asked Amanda. "Sure Amanda, it would probably be easier for me to draw it out and show you." Nick went off to get the whiteboard and pens from his office and Amanda decided it was an opportune time to make them all a drink. Nick returned and set the board up and then generally chatted with Brian until Amanda showed up with a tray of coffee mugs and some biscuits for them. They sat chatting whilst they sipped their drinks and ate a few biscuits. When they had finished Brian went over to the board, picked up the whiteboard marker pen and began to sketch.

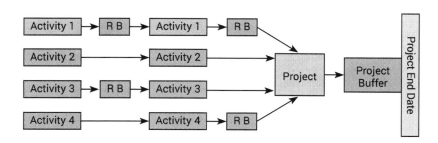

"Here we have our activities; one to four are the first set of activities that need to be done but as we move towards the second set of activities we find that we have an issue between one and five, and three and seven as they share the same resource buffer of RB. Whereas, the other activities do not have a hindrance and can proceed fairly easily. Therefore, we have to ensure that the resource buffers are well managed and that we do not turn them into multitasks. Activities two and six have no problems and flow through to the project. Hence these may be early finishers. We know that activities five and eight take longer because of the nature of the job; so, we put in a mini feeder buffer or FB. Should we need more time than allocated we have the main project buffer to pull time from, but if we have planned things right then we will finish the project before we use up all of the project buffer and so complete before the project's end date." Nick and Amanda studied the diagram and Nick nodded in approval, "I can see how this works and I am more confident than before that this refurbishment project will be done on or before time." "Me too, I can't wait to start" added Amanda. "Glad to see that you are both excited about this and feeling more positive. However, we still need to ensure that everyone in this team works together" "We already do" replied Nick. "I don't just mean you two, I mean the greater team which includes myself, Max your architect and his son, Dave and his building team, your suppliers, and anyone else that has an input into this project. "How is that accomplished?" Amanda asked. "I would rather wait until we have Dave and Max join us to explain about teamwork, as it would save me having to explain it twice and answering questions." Amanda was satisfied to wait, as she knew what it was like having to keep going over things. "So where do we go from here?" she asked. "Our next step is to start bringing the team together when we all meet up for the initial meeting with Dave and Max. In the meantime, you have plenty to be getting on with, so we can call it a day for now." Nick and Amanda agreed and with that, they said their goodbyes and Brian left for his office.

Chapter Eight

The week was busy for Nick and Amanda as they were working on their business to make the improvements that was suggested to them by Trevor and Brian. They actually found that the work was easier as they became more efficient and wondered why they had not done this several years before. Nick and Amanda were excited as the day of the meeting soon came around and now they could move onto the next stage.

Amanda was watering her small pot plant that was in the window of her living room when she saw Brian pull up in his car. She quickly finished watering her plant and called out to Nick to tell him as she went on her way to go and open the front door for him. Brian was just about to ring the bell when the door was opened by a smiling Amanda "Morning Brian," she greeted and gave him a kiss on each cheek. They went in and were soon joined by Nick who shook hands with Brian before they all settled down to wait for the others. Five minutes later, Dave showed up followed quickly by Max and his son Connor. They were shown to the living room by Amanda where she had coffee prepared for everyone and they introduced themselves, whilst sipping their drinks and settling down into their chairs. Brian got up and stood by the whiteboard, "Thank you for coming to this meeting. Nick and Amanda have appointed me as the project manager for the refurbishment of their property. The agenda for today is to talk a little about teamwork, as I need everyone one of you to work together on this project." Brian looked around the room at everybody to emphasise what he was saying. "Then we will go over to the property so that measurements, photographs, sketches etc. can be taken, and then we will meet back here for a closeout meeting and to allocate actions. Are there any questions so far?" Max pointed at the whiteboard, "That diagram looks familiar." They all looked towards the whiteboard, "That is one of the things I wanted to talk to you about. This diagram represents critical chain project management." Max nodded "I read about it a few years ago and it sounded interesting, but I have never seen it in action, so I am looking forward to see how it works." Brian then spent the next half an hour explaining the diagram, how critical chain works and what was expected from the team. "Right, as we have talked about what is expected from the team, this is a good opportunity to talk about teamwork. We need to have team-focused performance, so I expect everyone to express themselves and if you have any ideas or opinions we need to discuss them openly. I would rather that we have an argument at the start to clear the air and get your point across and commit to the project rather than keep things to yourself and then don't commit because you didn't agree. Any questions before I continue?" Dave rubbed his chin thoughtfully, "Are you saying that we work by team consensus?" "Good God no, consensus is a horrible way to run a business and we will definitely not be doing that. This is why I want you to argue your corner and use your passion and logic to make your point and I expect everyone to do this and to challenge each other until we have come up with the right answer." "Good, because if it is decisions by consensus you would have to find yourself another builder as I don't work that way." "Ok, I'm going to lay the ground rules. Everybody has to understand their own role and who is doing what so that there are no omissions. We have to ensure that there are contingency plans in place to cover all instances of individual's absence. Everyone must understand the metrics that we will put in place, as we will measure ourselves against them. As a minimum, we will have daily meetings to communicate where we are and if there are any problems that may need to be actioned. Are there any questions?" There was silence in the room as everyone absorbed what was said and thinking how it may affect them, then slowly they came to realise that the framework that had just been presented to them actually made sense and it was not arduous, so they could live with it. "I take from the lack of questions we are in agreement with this?" Brian asked as he looked around the room. Dave responded, "In theory, it all sounds good, I will hold judgement until we put it into practice." There were slight nods from some of the others "Fair enough, but I'm sure that you will see the benefits soon enough." "If we are finished here, Connor and I would like to take a look at the property so that we can get on with our preliminary designs." "I guess we are done here for the moment Max, so as you say let's get over to the property." They decided to travel in two cars, Max and Connor Joined Nick in his car, whilst Dave and Brian went with Amanda. Nick set off first whilst

Dave was getting a set of telescopic ladders out of his van, which he put, in Amanda's car boot before they set off along the back roads for a pleasant drive through the Warwickshire countryside to the property.

Half an hour later, they pulled up outside of the property and got out of the cars to view the property. Nick took out his keys and opened the door to let everyone into the property. Max and Connor stayed outside and took photographs of the building and roof before they went in. Dave, Max and Connor went straight upstairs where Dave took out his ladder, extended it up to the loft hatch, and as Connor held it steady, Dave went up and removed the hatch and put it out of the way before he pulled himself up and into the loft space. From his pocket he drew out a torch and switched it on then looked out onto Max and Connor, "Ok gentlemen, up you come." Max went up first and Dave gave him a hand up as he climbed into the loft space, he was soon followed by Connor. The three of them stood carefully on the joists as Dave shone his torch around the loft. The beam from the torch picked out the skeletal framework of the joists in the dark roof space. Max took out a small camera and started to take photographs. The flash from the camera brightly lit up the space and the three of them had to blink from being momentarily blinded by the flash. "I will just get some measurements and we are done here." Dave shone the torch along the joist that Connor was standing on so that he could see where he was walking, as he made his way towards the back wall where he took out a laser measuring tape, switched it on, held it up against the wall, and pointed it at the opposite wall. The narrow red beam hit the opposite wall and Connor took the reading and jotted it down. Connor did this at various parts of the roof space, including from floor to roof and slowly built up a picture with the data of measurements he had collected. Twenty minutes later, they had completed all of the measurements and climbed back down the ladder and onto the upstairs landing. "Are you happy that you have everything son?" "Yes dad, I have enough to produce a design so I'm happy." "Ok let's have a look around." Dave led them through the upstairs rooms as they looked to see where the best place would be to locate the stairs that they would need to build to go up into the loft. Connor took further measurements and photographs of the upstairs rooms before they went down stairs to meet with the others. "You all done upstairs?" Brian asked. "Yes, we have everything we need" replied Connor. "Is this an article four area?" Max asked Nick. "No, it's not, why do you ask?" "Well, as you will have a property that will have three floors after we have finished, I presumed that you were going to turn this property into an HMO." Nick glanced at Amanda before answering, "We hadn't thought about an HMO we just wanted to increase the done-up value of the house and make it more attractive for a higher rentable income from a single let. Do you think that this could be turned into an HMO?" "I don't see why not, it is just a box we can make it anything that you want within reason, but we would need to know before we start coming up with a design." "How much more would it cost?" "From our side we wouldn't charge you anymore for the design as it is easier for us starting out with a clean canvas." They all looked at Dave in anticipation of what he would say. Dave rubbed his chin and made some calculations in his head before answering, "I would think that as a minimum it would be at least five thousand more plus materials, but I can give you a more accurate figure once I have seen the design and know what is involved." "Fair enough, I guess it is down to me and Amanda to decide if we want an HMO. We will do the figures when we get back and then we can decide what we want." Amanda agreed "Yes we can do that; in the meantime, you may want to take measurements of the whole house in case we go ahead with it." Max and Connor went off to explore and measure the rest of the house and gardens. "I'm going to measure up the front to see how much fencing we will need to secure the site and find a location for the toilette and porta cabin." Dave left Brian, Nick and Amanda in the kitchen as he made his way to the front door. "What do you really think about the idea of an HMO?" Brian asked. "To be honest we have never done one before as it seems a bit more work to manage" replied Nick "It also feels daunting" Amanda chipped in. "Mmm, what you are really telling me is that it is outside of your comfort zone, so you really do not want to do it." Brian gaze flicked between Nick and Amanda and he stayed silent waiting to see who would speak first. Amanda gazed down to the floor as if suddenly finding it interesting; she could not put her finger on why she was nervous of going into HMOs. Nick was doing the opposite, gazing into space trying to come up with a logical answer, and failing miserably before finally admitting to himself that Brian was right. "Ok, we are out of our comfort zone; we have shied away from it because it sounds so hard to manage." "Nick it's like anything, so long as you have your systems in place to minimise your risks then it shouldn't be a problem to you." "I guess." From Nick's short answer, Brian knew there was more than just the management of an HMO that was worrying them both. "I have the feeling that there is something else that is also holding you back." Again, there was silence for a few moments, and this time it was Amanda that needed to fill the void "The rules and regulations for an HMO look like a real nightmare to understand." "I understand where you are coming from, regulations can look daunting at first glance but like anything else, once you get to understand them then it will be so much easier, but remember you are not doing this on your own." "With respect Brian, you don't know anything about HMO regulations" Nick replied. "You are right, I don't. However, you have a builder and an architect who do." Nick now looked sheepish "I'm sorry, you are right." "No problem Nick, stepping out of your comfort zone produces reluctance and fear that it will cloud your judgement. Whereas, if we break it all down into small chunking steps we can get through things with logic." "How do you mean?" asked Amanda. "Let me ask you a question, what is your greatest fear?" Amanda thought about it "I think it would be having to do a presentation." "That is a good example, so let's think about it for a minute; if you did a presentation then it would be because you were subject matter expert or SME, so you would know your subject inside out. Yes?" "Well I suppose so," replied Amanda reluctantly. "So, questions would not faze you as you would be able to answer the majority of the questions. Because you are, the SME people will be listening to you, as they want to learn, so they will be on your side. Yes?" "Yes" Amanda nodded. "Therefore, you are not going to be heckled, so with everyone on your side and knowing your subject that you are passionate about means that you will have greater confidence. Do you agree?" "When you put it like that then yes." "Tell me, now that we have gone through your fear with logic what is there to be afraid of?" "Well I suppose there is nothing really." Amanda was quite surprised at herself as she replayed Brian's conversation over again in her mind and found that she did feel that she could go and present to an audience. "So, does an HMO faze you now?" "No, I don't think that it does." "Does that mean that you and Nick will now consider turning this property into an HMO?" Amanda and Nick looked at each other and nodded "If the figures stack up then yes, we will turn this into an HMO" replied Nick with greater confidence than he had felt just a few minutes earlier.

Dave came back in and joined Brian, Nick and Amanda in the kitchen. "Dave have you done an HMO before?" asked Nick. "Yes, I have done about half a dozen of them." "That's great, so you know the regulations for an HMO?" "Well yes, I do. However, each council may have their own requirements, so you have to talk to the local environmental officer as that is the person that decides everything. I have found that in the past, if you involve the environmental officer from the start then things will go easier and you will have no problem obtaining your HMO licence." "Thank you, Dave, that is good information that I wasn't really aware of, and it is good to know that you have experience." Dave nodded his head slightly in acknowledgement, and then looked up "Here are the lads." Max and Connor stepped into the kitchen from the rear garden "We are finished, so we can make a move whenever you're ready." "Ok Max, if you guys make your way out I will just lock up. Amanda I will see you back home." They all made their way out of the house and Brian, Amanda and Dave got into Amanda's car and headed back.

They all sat having drinks in the living room generally chatting and getting to know each other. Nick took his tablet out and began to run the numbers on his spreadsheet to see if the HMO was viable. "How many rooms do you think that we could get in the property for an HMO?" Nick asked Max. Max turned to Connor "What do you think?" Connor took his notepad out of his messenger bag and went through his measurements. "Six would be comfortable, but I can get eight, but it will be a squeeze." Nick used the information to enter the numbers into his spreadsheet. Brian discreetly watched with interest and wondered which way Nick would go; would it be maximising the profit or think about his customers and think about their comforts and needs he thought. Ten minutes later Nick looked up and asked to be excused, as he needed to have a quick chat with Amanda. They went to their office and closed the door "I have done the figures, for a six bed we will get a cash flow of one thousand three hundred pounds a month, which is with one room factored in as a void and interest rate higher than what it is currently as a stress test. If we go to an eight bed then our cash flow will be two thousand and sixty-five pounds per month, with the same stress test." "Wow that is a big difference to what we were getting with a buy to let." "Yes, it is, so are you happy to go down this route?" Amanda took just a moment to think about it. "Yes, I think that we need to have a go, because if we don't we will always be thinking what if." "I agree, so which way do you want to go, a six or eight bedroom?" "What are your thoughts?" Amanda countered. Nick took a deep breath before he answered "Although the extra seven hundred and sixty-five pounds we would gain from an eight bed would be useful, I don't think we should go down that route. This is simply because I want long term tenants, so they need to be comfortable with enough space, so I want it to appeal to professional people. So, in effect I'm thinking of a short-term loss to get a long-term gain." Amanda was amazed, was this was not the Nick of just a few months ago; he had changed for the better. She went over to him, hugged, and kissed him. "So proud of you Hun, let's tell the others." They went back into the living room and everyone stopped talking as they waited in anticipation for Nick and Amanda to say something. Nick stood in the centre of the room and faced everyone "We have decided that we would like to build a six-bedroom HMO." Brian nodded in approval. "We will base our plans on your decision and come up with a design for your approval" said Connor. Nick sat back down with a look of relief on his face. Brian got up and stood by the whiteboard "How familiar are you all with CDM twenty fifteen?" he asked. Max was the first to reply, "We are totally conversant with it, as we have to be in our line of work." Brian turned to Dave and thought that he would not be surprised if Dave did not know about the regulations so between him, Max and Connor he would have to teach him. "As the principle contractor I know what my responsibilities are under CDM twenty fifteen." Dave smiled as he said it, as he knew that they were not expecting it from a small building company. Brian could not help but smile at Dave's response both from relief that he knew about the regulations and by the deadpan way, that Dave said it. "Well that is great news that is something else we can tick off the list that we don't have to worry about." Brian then pointed at Dave, Connor and Max "I need you three to do something that you don't normally do. I want you to work together to come up with the design." Max and Connor looked shocked, but Dave didn't seem fazed and just smiled. "Brian, I need to understand your thought process, as normally we would come up with the design and once approved we will produce detailed drawings and pass them onto the contractor." "Calm down Connor, I will explain it to you. Suppose that, instead of a business we are a football team. I am the manager and you are the team. Now I call you all into the dressing room, I go into my office, I call you in one at a time, and I explain to everyone individually what the tactic is and what your role is. We then go out onto the pitch against our opponents and get absolutely annihilated. The reason for it was that none of you knew what each other was supposed to be doing because you didn't hear what was being said to your team mates so none of you could see the bigger picture. I want you three to work together because between you, there is experience to come up with something that is elegant and practical. It will also mean that the refurbishment will go quicker as most of the work will have been done at the planning stage by you three." "I have no problem with working with these two" replied Dave. Max and Connor were quiet for a few moments as they try to think of why it would not be a good idea and they realised that they could not come up with a logical reason; it was just the traditional way it had always been. "Ok, I can work with Dave." "Me too" replied Connor. "Thank you, gentlemen, how long do you think it will take to come up with your initial design?" "About two weeks for the initial" replied Connor. Brian looked at him "Remember what I asked for when we were discussing critical chain. Now I am going to ask you again, how long will it take to do the initial design?" Colour ran to Connor's cheeks with embarrassment "Sorry, old habits die hard, I think it can be done in a week." Brian looked at Max to confirm this and Max nodded his head in agreement. "Thank you, Connor, but as you can see just by being honest we have already saved fifty percent of the time that traditionally will have been filled up with other things." The group agreed, and Nick and Amanda having seen Brian starting to work as project manager were now feeling very confident that Brian would help bring this project on time and on budget. "With regards to payment for this project this is how it is going to work. Nick and Amanda are going to set up an escrow account." Nick raised his hand "Sorry Brian, but for my benefit can you explain what an escrow account is." "Basically, it is a separate account where money is deposited for the project, both you and this team know that the money is there, and at certain stages when both sides are satisfied money is released. This not only protects you as the customer as you can ensure that everything is running smoothly and there are no extra hidden costs, but it also protects the team as they know they will get paid as you cannot pull out and leave them high and dry. Does that answer your question?" "Yes, thank you." "As part of the payment there will be a penalty clause if the project goes over time, and before you say anything Dave; this is for the agreed work at the start of the project. If Nick and Amanda want to make changes during the project then that is an extra, so it will not count on the timeline." Dave was satisfied that this had been taken into consideration; as in his experience clients changed their minds over things and still wanted done on time and it has not been possible so it has led to unnecessary arguments. "By the same token, if the project comes under time there will be a bonus, after all it is only fair that if you come below the target timeline then you should be rewarded." "What sort of figures have you got in mind for penalty and bonus?" asked Amanda. "As a penalty it would be your day rate plus three percent per day, and as a bonus it would be your day rate plus three percent per day saved. Does that sound fair?" "Well we will have the design done quickly so we will hit our target" replied Connor. Dave was about to say something, but Brian spoke first. "Sorry Connor but I'm going to disappoint you, we are not working in silos where once you have done your bit you throw it over the wall and forget about it. This is about teamwork, so it is getting the whole team over the line, so we have to work together." Dave smiled, as normally it would be his building team that would be in the firing line, so all of the pressure would be on him. As it was now a team effort, they would all share the responsibility for finishing the project on time. "But once we have done our bit we are done" persisted Connor. Max just looked on with mild amusement to see who was going to win this argument as he knew that his son could be headstrong and stubborn, so it will be interesting to see how Brian was going to deal with it. "Sorry Connor, but you will not be done as you put it, you are the principle designer therefore you are responsible for ensuring that the build conforms to your design as well as to regulations. That makes you the subject matter expert and therefore a major part of this team." "But I am not responsible for the actual build, so I should not be penalised for lateness." "You are wrong, you are responsible for the build too, as Dave and his crew may find that they cannot build what you have specified as you may have not thought of the practicalities. Also, as I said earlier teamwork is crucial for this project. Consequently, I expect everyone to not only pull their weight but to also help out where it is needed. Therefore, I need to know whether you are on board or not." The atmosphere in the room suddenly changed as they waited for Connor to reply. Connor's mind was now in turmoil, part of him wanted to rebel and walk away from the project, whilst the other part of him wanted this project to show his dad that he was ready to take over the business. He looked across at his dad looking for some sign that would help make up his mind, but Max had a poker face, so he knew that the decision was his and his alone. He noticed that all conversation in the room had stopped and everyone was watching him to see what he would say. He thought back to his time when he was studying to be an architect and told everyone that he was going to make a difference and not be a traditional architect like everyone else, and he suddenly saw the quote from Albert Einstein that used to be on his lecturer's desk that said the definition of insanity was doing the same thing over and over again and expecting a different result. He took a deep breath "Looks like we will be working as a team." Nick let out a breath, he had not realised that he had been holding it until that point. Brian was happy that the challenge had come early, as he wanted to set out his stall and ensure that everyone understood that he was in charge as the project manager. "Ok gentlemen we are agreed on payment; the only thing left to do now is to decide when you will actually start on the design." Max looked pointedly at Connor "We can make a start tomorrow." "Dave and I will come over to your office to go through it with you, so we will be there at about nine o'clock." "Here is our card, the address is on it." "Thank you. Dave what time shall I pick you up?" Dave rubbed his chin "Eight o'clock, I will write down my address before we leave." "Gentlemen we will be having daily meetings throughout this project, when we get on site, the meetings will also include all trades." "Why trades, they will do as I tell them" replied Dave. "Dave, I need everyone engaged. Some of your team may have ideas that we can implement, I want them to help and work with each other and I don't want a them and us culture. As I said before, teamwork is crucial, so they will be involved." Connor smiled as he saw Dave's discomfort at being challenged. Dave saw Connor's smile from the corner of his eye, so he put on a smile, "Ok boss, no problem." Connor stopped smiling. Dave saw it and thought if Connor was going to see him have an argument over something that was trivial and not worth fighting for he was very much mistaken. By acknowledging that Brian was in charge he had shown Connor that he would stand by Brian. Brian too had noticed Connor watching Dave and therefore wanted to acknowledge his cooperation as soon as Dave agreed to the daily meetings. "Thank you, Dave, your cooperation is very much appreciated." Dave gave a slight nod as if to say your welcome. Amanda was fascinated as she saw the team dynamics change as Brian started to use his authority to bind the team to the project and make that the focus rather than on individuals. Amanda decided that this would be a good time for them to do a little bonding. Hence, she announced that she would be serving lunch and she could do with a hand. Max was the first to respond, "How can I help?" "Can you clear the table please? Nick can you bring out the food, Brian can you help him please. Connor there is a tablecloth in the top left-hand draw of the sideboard over there. Dave you have the hardest job; you can just take it easy as everything is covered." They all jumped up to do her bidding. You are not the only one that can lead a team Brian she thought with a smile. The table was soon laid with a buffet and drinks for everyone, and they started to help themselves and began to chat as they ate and so got to know each other a bit more. Amanda was chatting with Dave and found out that he had been in the Royal Air Force for twenty years, which struck a chord with her as her father too had been in the air force. So, they ended up comparing notes on the RAF camps that they had lived on and found that they had a couple in common although each were there at different times. Nick was talking to Max and found out that he too had been in the forces but this time it was the army where he was an officer in the Royal Engineers for fifteen years. This is where he also learnt to become an architect in readiness to be a civilian again. Brian and Connor found that they were both martial artists, with Brian being a third Dan black belt in Aikido and Connor being a first Dan black belt in Tae Kwon Do.

They finished having lunch and cleared all of the food away and thanked Nick and Amanda for the spread. "Nick, I want you to start thinking about the materials that we may need and make a list, we will give you greater details once we have finalised the design and start to spec it. However, you can look at things that we will need such as smoke alarms, lighting, carbon monoxide alarms, fire blankets etc." Nick made a note of his task. Later, he would create a spreadsheet for the list. "Amanda can you get in touch with the environmental officer and explain what we are doing and get his advice, I suggest that you build up a relationship as the officer will be key to this project." "Ok Brian, I will call him tomorrow and make an appointment to see him as soon as possible." Brian pulled out a folder, took out some papers, and gave everyone a copy. "Here are the RACI diagrams that I have prepared for you." Once he had handed them out he went through it and explained how the RACI diagram worked. Max was the first to speak "I like the way that this works because now nobody can hide from their responsibilities, I wish that I had known about this years ago it would have saved a lot of time on arguments." Dave nodded in agreement "I can definitely make use of this with the trades as they often argue that they weren't aware of what needed doing or who was doing it, which in reality were just excuses so now there is no getting away with it, so thank you for showing and explaining this to us." "You're welcome, glad that you have taken this on board and ready to use it. Right I think that unless anyone else has something that they want to discuss we are done for the day." The group looked around at each other to see if anyone would speak and when it came apparent no one would Dave got up to leave and the others followed suit and said their goodbyes as they got into their vehicles.

It was five to eight when Brian knocked on Dave's front door a few minutes later the door opened, and Dave stood there. "Morning Brian, glad to see that you are punctual, one of my pet hates tardiness." "Morning Dave, if you're ready then let's go." Brian stepped back to let Dave out. Dave closed and locked the door behind him and followed Brian down his garden path and out of the gate, which Dave closed, and down to the car. They climbed in and Brian programmed his satnav and put in the address that was on the business card that he had been given, and they set off to Kenilworth. "Well Dave what do you think of working with architects at the design stage?" Dave thought about it for a moment "It will be a novelty as I don't normally see plans until afterwards, however I can see the logic of working with them from the start, as they are good at the theory and making it all look pretty but they don't have to build it, so they don't realise the problems and delays it can cause, so I am really looking forward to this and putting in my two penneth worth." Brian smiled "I understand where you are coming from, it is not often that you can have an input at the start of a project, but I know that your experience is valuable to the success of this project, which is why I have brought you in right at the start and I want you involved as much as possible." "No problem there, although some say I'm quiet because I listen and take it all in, I will shout out if I believe that something is fundamentally wrong."

Before long they found themselves on the outskirts of Kenilworth and heading towards the Elizabethan castle of the same name, before heading off to Red Lane. Ten minutes later, they pulled into a drive of a large detached house that was set off the road. They could see a large stone terrace area with tables and chairs, with Max sitting in one of the chairs. He looked up from the paper that he was reading and waved to them. Brian and Dave got out of the car and Max shouted down to them to come up the stairs at the side of the building to join him on the terrace. They shook hands and Max offered them drinks as they waited for Connor to join them. "Nice place that you have here." Thank you, Brian, I will show you around later, it is a six bedroom and it has an indoor swimming pool and gym. We converted the stable block to an office and that is where we work from." "It must be worth a bob or two then." Dave remarked. "One and a half million," replied Connor as he stepped out onto the terrace to join the other. Brian and Dave shook hands with him, and the three of them followed Connor to his and Max's glass fronted office. The office was light and airy with very light grey painted walls apart from a feature wall that was painted burgundy red. There were tasteful watercolour paintings on the grey walls and pictures and sketches of properties on the burgundy wall. The light was mainly natural as it came not only through the glass front but also from skylights. The office furniture was contemporary, tasteful in its design, and so fitted perfectly with the theme and layout of the office. "This is the main part of the office where we receive clients and potential clients." "Very nice Max, it looks welcoming and impressive, so it shows what sort of standard you work to." "Thank you, Brian." Connor went to a door at the end of the room and opened it and went through it, the others followed him into a short corridor "Toilets are through that door there." Connor pointed to a door on his left-hand side and continued to the door at the end of the corridor where he opened it and they stepped into an equally impressive office space but more functional. The walls in this area had whiteboards, a smart board and a large screen hung on them.

There were several computer monitors on desks and a large printer stood in the corner alongside stood a bookshelf. Connor spread out his arms "This is where the magic happens, this is our workspace and where we get down to the nuts and bolts." Brain and Dave stood and looked around taking it all in. "Come sit here," Max indicated to some chairs around a long solid oak table. They sat down and found themselves looking at the large screen. Connor switched his computer on and turned on the large screen. "You can watch the model come together as I build it with the software from the measurements that we took" Connor explained. As Connor built up the floorplan, he began to change it into a 3D model on the screen. Max explained to Brian and Dave what Connor was doing and how it worked. Connor printed off the floor plans and the pictures that he had taken of the house and placed them on the table in front of the others before going back to his computer. "Ok this is the original house, now I am going to make the changes to turn it into an HMO." They watched the screen, saw walls disappear, and rebuilt in other places and en-suite going in to each bedroom and then the lot conversion with stairs being relocated. "What do you think?" Connor asked with obvious pride in his voice. Dave studied the photos before him and compared them to what was on the screen. Brian turned to Connor "You obviously have a good eye and feel for this because it looks impressive." Connor was pleased with the praise he had just received. "You need to move the en-suite to the opposite side," said Dave as he once more compared the photos to the model on the screen. Before he could continue, Connor interrupted him. "No, if I do that it will spoil the feel of the rooms" replied Connor with just a touch of anger in his voice. "You still need to move them." "I will not, there is no need, are you not listening it will spoil the feel of the rooms." Brian stood up "Gentlemen before this gets out of hand I think we need to understand why Dave has made that comment." "If you look at the outside pipes for drainage you will see that they are on the opposite side of the room to the en-suite. Therefore, to keep the en-suite where they are it would mean an extra cost because the floorboards would have to come up, extra pipe would have to be laid and there is always the risk that the pipe may leak, so the future maintenance cost would be quite high." Connor and Max looked at the photos of the house and saw that Dave was right. "I'm sorry for my outburst Dave, I should have spotted that." "No hard feelings, we all make mistakes lad, but at least it was on paper and not on the actual build, so you can fix it." "Yes, you're right, I will reconfigure the model." Brian nodded and knew it was the right decision to bring Dave in at the start of the project. Connor worked away for the next few hours trying to get the design right so that it was practical and pleasing. Max in the meantime made sketches of the outside of the house to design the kerb appeal. They decided to break for lunch and as it was such a nice day, they decided to have lunch on the outside terrace where Max and Connor brought out salad and a selection of cheeses and ham, small bread rolls and poured them out a glass of white wine each. They chatted as they ate and got to know each other better. There was a friendly banter and ribbing between Dave and Max when they discovered they had both been in the forces. So, of course, the conversation was about which one of the forces was best and scoring points off each other and laughing about it as only veterans can. After lunch they continued with the design, each area of the model was closely checked, and minor changes had to be made when, on a couple of occasions, Dave spotted a problem that needed to be addressed. Although it was more work for Connor, he began to appreciate Dave's experience and attention to detail and realised that working with a builder at the start of the project was not a bad idea after all. Several hours later, they completed the initial design and were all happy with the outcome. Copies were printed off and they checked a final time before declaring satisfaction. Brian stood and addressed the others, "Gentlemen I will take this to our client and get their view of the design and see if they want to make any changes. More importantly, by working together and dealing with potential snags we have completed this initial design in a day, so we have potentially saved a week on the project." "I estimated a week because normally the initial design will go back and forth between us and the client." replied Connor. "That may still happen. However, looking at what has been produced, I don't think it will be the case in this instance." "I agree Brian, so I think that Connor and I can get on with provisionally looking at the scheme of works. Dave, would you like to join us for this tomorrow?" There was no hesitation from Dave "Sure Max, same time as today?" he replied. "Yes, nine o'clock will be just fine, unless you want to come a bit earlier and join us for breakfast first." Dave thought about it for a second "See you for mess call at half past eight." There were smiles all round as they bid their farewells; it had been a long but productive day.

Brian had called Nick on his way home and made arrangements to call in the next day with a copy of the plans. At nine o'clock Brian was knocking on Nick's door. When the door opened, Amanda stood before him, greeted him, and invited him in. They went to the now familiar living room where Nick was waiting. Once they had settled down with a drink each, Brian took the plans out from a leather folder that he had been carrying. "Well, this is what you have been waiting to see." He opened the plan out and laid it on the table before them. Nick and Amanda were quiet as they took it in and studied all the details. Nick was the first to break the silence. "Wow, it is better than I was expecting as I didn't realise each room would have its own en-suite." Brian smiled, "This is why Connor asked if you want it comfortable or squeezed with extra rooms. In my opinion, you went with the right decision as now you will appeal to professional people." "That means I can plan the décor so that it will appeal to that group," Chipped in Amanda feeling excited. "Yes, you can and if you make it appealing enough that you create demand, then you could possibly charge a little bit more, so you could come close to the eight bed HMO that you considered." "You're right, I hadn't thought of that," replied Nick. "Now that you have had an initial look at the design, I want you to look at them again but this time with a critical eye. This is because; if there is something that you don't like, it is easy to change at this stage. Once we get into the build it will be more difficult." Brian got up from the table and sat in an armchair, pulled out his tablet and began to check his emails whilst Nick and Amanda reviewed the design.

Twenty minutes later, Nick and Amanda decided that they had seen enough. "I am quite happy to go with this design." "Me too," added Amanda. "Ok guys, I will ring Max and let him know that you're happy to run with it." Brian pulled out his mobile phone and rang Max. "Hi Max, I'm with Nick and Amanda, they have reviewed the design and are happy to run with it. Yes, Max that is good news, how is it going with the scheme of works?" Brian listened carefully as Max explained. "That is great Max, I'm so glad that Dave has been a big help. Can you and Dave continue with that whilst Connor starts with the detailed plans? Thank you. Let me know when it's done so that we can begin to arrange for the material to be on site. Talk to you later Max, bye." Brian hung up and explained what Max had told him to Nick and Amanda. "I can't believe that we are nearly ready to start, I am so excited, I can't wait." Brian and Nick smiled at Amanda's enthusiasm. She was unconsciously moving side to side from one foot to another like a little girl about to receive her first puppy. "Have you set up an escrow account?" Brian asked. "I spoke to the bank and they put me in touch with the people that set it up for me, so we are ready to go." Nick replied. "What about you Amanda, have you spoken to the environmental officer?" "Yes, I spoke to him briefly on the phone and I have an appointment with him this afternoon so that he can tell me what is expected from us, so having these drawings today is great timing." "Nick have you started making a list of the materials that we will need?" "Yes, I have put everything in a spreadsheet and as soon as I get the details from Dave and the guys I will add it in." Brian was pleased, as everything for the first phase was coming together and the project was already ahead of time. "Well done. When I have the information from the guys, I will forward it to you so that we can start to get the supplies that we will need. For the moment, just carry on with your jobs until you hear from me." "Thanks Brian for getting this moving quickly and for all your help up to now." "You're welcome Nick. Ok I better be off as I have a meeting to attend to, let me know if you get stuck with anything." Brian gathered his things and bade Nick and Amanda farewell.

Chapter Nine

A few days later, Brian received a call from Connor to say they had completed the detailed drawings and the scheme of work. Brian was very pleased as it meant that the project was now ahead of time. Connor also gave him some news that surprised him. It turned out that Dave had been key in helping them get ahead as he had an eye for the details and Connor and Max were quite impressed with him and realised he would be an asset, so they had offered to merge with his company on an equal partnership which he had accepted. So now they could offer a complete service from design to build. In the little time that he had got to know Dave, he was impressed with him and liked him hence, he was glad to see that his talents were appreciated by others. He asked Connor to send a copy of the detailed plans and scheme of works to Nick, and then arranged for them to meet up in a couple of days. Brian then called Nick and explained what he had learnt from Connor and asked him to get Amanda to show the environmental officer a copy of the plans, as he wanted to make sure at the early stage the officer was on board with what they were doing. Because, when it comes to final planning they would have an ally.

A couple of days later they all met up at Nick and Amanda's house. Brian was the first to arrive quickly followed by Dave then Max and Connor arrived a few minutes later. Drinks were served by Amanda and they settled down ready for their meeting. Brian got up "Thank you for your attendance, we will start with a recap." Brian was more business-like in conducting this meeting. "The design was completed and approved. The detailed drawings and scheme of works have now been completed. The environmental officer is now on board, and because of the effort that had been put into the initial work, the environmental officer has not asked for any changes. The materials list has been started and because of your efforts we are ahead of schedule, so well done." The others looked at each other and there were smiles all around. "Now we have reached the next stage. Things will start to get busy and normally, the pressure will start to build up and the stress levels will rise, and this is where I come in. I will of course drive this project and I will push you all but only to a level of healthy stress." "Excuse me Brian, what do you mean by healthy stress?" asked Connor. The others leaned forward in their chairs, as they too wanted to know the answer. "When we look at human performance there are three levels of stress. These are: under stressed, overstressed and healthy stress. Under stressed is where you have things such as insufficient work, lack of direction, repetitive monotonous work, you don't get feedback and basically, you are unmotivated. Therefore, boredom sets in and very little gets done and the quality of the work is generally poor. Then we have the other extreme, which is overstressed. This is where we have things such as unrealistic timescales, giving people complex tasks to do without the training, asking people to do tasks without the proper tools, people not being supported, there could also be bullying and discrimination. What we are looking for in healthy stress is for it to fall in between the two extremes by having things such as sensible timescales, good communications, a steady but challenging workload, be well supported etc." "I can see where you're coming from, but I thought that all stress is unhealthy" replied Connor. "That is a myth, there are positive effects of stress so long as it is healthy stress and it includes acceleration of the activities of the brain, improvement in the quality of immediate decisions, it also helps speed up decision making. You will become more alert and it will also improve your memory." "Brian's right. In the forces we find this all the time. We can go right the way through the three types of stresses in minutes depending on what we were doing, but most of the time we were at the healthy stress range as this is when we were most effective. Your dad, of course by being a Rupert was mainly under stressed." Dave smiled as he made the last comment. Max laughed and good humouredly replied "Just for those of you that don't understand, a Rupert is the name that the ranks of the British Army give to officers, but in particular to officers who has an upper-middle or upper-class background and has a total lack of skills or common sense." The others chuckled. "Just to make it clear, and despite what Dave thinks, I am no Rupert." There was more laughter especially when Dave shook his head with a look of disbelief on his face. When the laughter died down Brian brought them back to the meeting. "Dave, when can you secure the site?" "I have everything ready, so I can have it secured tomorrow, with fencing and security cameras." "Great, go ahead and secure it. Whilst Dave is securing the site Connor can you work with Nick and complete the materials list?" "Yes of course, we should have that completed by tomorrow." "It would be good if you did as we can get started quickly. Amanda can you create some budget check sheets, one overall check sheet and the others detailed for the work that is being carried out." "Can you give me an idea of what you mean?" asked Amanda. Brian went over to the whiteboard and taking up a whiteboard marker pen began to draw out a table. "The first table contains all of the phases," Brian then drew another table. "This second table takes one of the phases and breaks it down further, so that you have more detail."

Phase	Budget Costs			Actual Costs		
	Labour	Materials	Total	Labour	Materials	Total
Design Costs						
Preliminaries						
Masonry Work						
Flooring						
Roof Structure						
Roof						
Doors & Windows						
Plumbing						
Electrics						
Joinery						
Plastering						
Heating						
Floor Coverings						
Decoration						
Bathroom						
Kitchen						
External Works						
Landscaping						

Phase Breakdown

Phase	Cost Item	Quantity	Unit	Budget Costs				Actual Costs				Difference
				Labour	Material	Equipment	Total	Labour	Material	Equipment	Total	
Masonry	Bricks											
	Inner skin Blockwork											
	Outer skin cladding											
	Steel Beams											
	Wall Plate											
	Concrete Lintels											
	Cavity Wall Insulation											
	Miscellaneous											

"What is unit?" Amanda asked. "Unit refers to the unit of measurement that is used to buy the material, such as metres, metres squared etc. When you calculate your budget cost, you use the unit of measure that you buy it for and multiply it by the quantity. You can then compare this with the actual costs as the build goes on." Brian wrote down an example on the board just to illustrate it.

Beam Unit = Metres, Cost = £5 per Metre, Estimated requirement = 50 Metres, Total Cost = £250

Actual Requirement = 60 Metres, Actual Total Cost £300.

Actual Cost – Estimated Cost = £300 - £250 = £50 Difference

"This will help not only in this build but also in future builds as you will have a better idea of what the costs could be as you will be better informed." "I can see how useful it would be in the future, especially as it is broken down in phases This will allow us to pick the phase that is most suitable to what we are doing," Amanda replied. "Eventually you will build up a library and be able to estimate a job with a high degree of accuracy" Max added. "It also means that rogue trades won't be able to pull the wool over your eyes as you will have an idea of labour rates, how long a job can take and what materials would be required" Dave also added. "That will cut your profits Dave" Max quipped, getting his own back for the earlier remark made by Dave about being a Rupert. The others chuckled at the remark. "Dave I will meet you onsite tomorrow, once you have it secured we will start work on the property." "Ok boss, I will make sure that my crew is ready." "Well, you all know what you need to do, so unless someone else has something they would like to add I will end this meeting." Brian looked around the room, but no one spoke "Ok, thank you for your time". The team broke up and said their farewells.

Dave was onsite at seven o'clock in the morning supervising the unloading of steel fencing that was going to be used to secure the site. The large portable cabin that would become the office, canteen and changing room with shower for the duration of the project had already been delivered. Brian pulled up onsite just as the last of the fencing was secured in place. "Morning Dave." "Morning boss, as you can see the site is now secure as far as fencing goes, the lads are just going to set up some security cameras then we will be ready to start work." "Good work Dave, I take it that we have electrics to the office" Brian asked. "Yes, we do, that was the first job that we did this morning." "Great, I'm going set up my laptop, and stick the kettle on." "Good idea, I will join you in a minute." Brian went off to get himself acquainted with his new office whilst Dave explained to his team where he wanted the cameras situated. Brian was surprised at the room that he had available in the cabin; he opened a door and walked through into the canteen area, then went through to another door where he found a changing room with ten lockers, a shower room and a toilet. The cabin was clean, and the walls were painted white that made it look even bigger. He walked down a narrow corridor to another door that led to the office. The office and the canteen had large windows that let in a lot of natural light that reflected off the white interior and made the cabin look light and airy. Brian set his laptop up on one of four grouped desks that had sockets recessed into the back of the desk. Each of the desks had low blue dividers that could be used to pin notes, drawings etc. and gave a small amount of privacy in what was an open office. Brian then went into the canteen and filled the kettle with water and switched it on. Dave appeared just as Brian was pouring the hot water into the mugs to make coffee. "Your timing is perfect Dave." "I do my best, so what do you think of your new home?" "It is better than I expected, but the first thing we are going to do is ditch the kettle in favour of an industrial hot water dispenser, that way there is no waiting around for hot water for drinks, so it means less time waiting in the canteen." "Good idea, and while you're at it buy a fast-hot air hand dryer so your hands are dry in ten seconds or less as this will save us money on hand towels and again saves time." "I like your thinking; I'm glad that we are on the same page." They wandered into the office and Dave took out a set of plans and taped them to the wall so that they were in plain view. He then took out a permanent marker and in bold black letters he wrote the date and issue number on the blank corner of the drawing. Then on a whiteboard, he took a whiteboard marker and wrote the same information on the board. Brian looked on and then asked, "Why have you written on the drawing and the board?" "In my experience, changes happen due to unforeseen circumstances; therefore, drawings can change so I always mark up the drawings and put the same information on the board so that everyone knows what they are supposed to be working on. If there is any discrepancy between the two it should be questioned." "I like that idea; it is a good example of visual management." "I just know that it saves time and money as costly mistakes are avoided if everyone knows what they are working on. My crew will check the drawing at least twice a day not only for information but also to make sure that there are no changes." There was a knock at the door and a head appeared around the door, "Where do you want the monitors set up Dave?" Dave pointed to one of the desks. "Put them there Mike." Mike set the monitors down on the desk and began to set them up. "Mike, let me introduce you to Brian." Mike looked up, took a couple of steps towards Brian, and thrust out his hand. Brian shook Mike's hand and felt the crush of a strong grip. "Hi Mike, I'm Brian and I am the project manager for this build, so you will be seeing a lot of me." Mike smiled but glanced across to Dave who nodded perceptively. "Nice to meet you Brian, I'm sure we will get along just fine." "Mike as well as being my brick layer is my right-hand man, so if I am not about and you need something done talk to him." "I will bear that in mind. I suppose that this is as good a time as any to meet the rest of your team." "Round the guys up Mike, and don't dawdle." Mike went off to get the rest of the team whilst Brian and Dave walked through to the canteen, as there was more room than the office for a meeting. A few minutes later Mike and the rest of Dave's team appeared and stood waiting for the introductions. Dave introduced Brian to his team and as he gave their names, Brian shook hands with them. "This is Joe; he is our carpenter. Derek is the plasterer. Pete is our electrician and Jeff is our plumber. Brian is the project manager for this build, and later on you will meet the architects Max and Connor" "You will also be seeing a lot of the owners, Nick and Amanda as they are going to be actively involved," Brian added. There were a few glances towards Dave from his team to see if he would object or say anything about this, but when he remained quiet, they accepted it. "We are going to have two stand up meetings a day, one in the morning before we start work and one in the afternoon straight after lunch. The meetings will be used to discuss what we are doing, how we are progressing, any issues and any opportunities for improvements. I need all of you to actively participate in these meetings as it is just not my meeting it is a team meeting." "I would like to add to that" Dave said. "You know my attitude to getting things done and getting it right, I just expect it to be done and I did not hold many meetings but having participated in some of these meetings I have found it surprisingly useful. So, during these meetings don't hold back and say what you think." "Thank you, Dave. During these meetings I will be challenging the status quo and I will be pushing everyone, but I won't overstress you, it is my job to get this project done on time and on budget but I cannot do this on my own, so I need everyone on board. If you see something that is wrong, shout up. If you can see a way of doing things better don't keep it to yourself, tell us about it so that it can be considered. Although I may be in charge of this project it does not mean to say that, I know everything, because I don't. I am just as reliant on you as you are on me, so we have to work as a team as it will be the only way we can get this project done." "Brian is right, and I can say that from first-hand experience, I worked with the architects to help with the design and the details we did it in a quarter of the time that it would normally take, and we ironed out some issues right at the start to make our job easier and to reduce some of the costs. There are a couple of things that I haven't told you yet, so this is a good time as any to make an announcement. You are all going to get a pay rise because I have amalgamated the company with the architect's company as equal partners so now we can offer a complete service from design to build, so it means that we will get more work and we can grow as a company. Day to day work will not change, so you will not notice much of a difference. It just means that there are more directors, I will introduce you to them when they are onsite. Secondly, for this project if we bring it under time you will get a three percent bonus per day saved, so it is very much in our interest to get this done fast but without cutting any corners as it has to be good quality work." "Excuse me boss, does this mean that the share scheme that you were considering for us is no longer on the table?" Mike asked. "I can tell you now that the scheme is very much on the table, it has already been discussed and agreed, we just need to do the legal bits for it to happen." There was a collective sigh and then a buzz as they started to talk among themselves. "I haven't finished yet." The room quickly quietened as the team waited to hear what Dave had to say. "As I was saying, you will get a bonus if we save days. However, if we go over then we will be hit with a penalty clause which means that it will come out of the company profits, therefore out of your pockets as future shareholders. As Brian has already said we need to work together as a team to make this happen." "Right guys, as we are all gathered here get yourselves a drink and food if you need it, then I will introduce you to our metrics board." The team started to take off their hard hats and organised themselves, to get their drinks and breakfast sorted out, whilst Dave went into the office and Brian went over to his car. Brian returned a few minutes later with a large black zipped case, the type that artists use to carry about their work and began setting up the paperwork that was in the case.

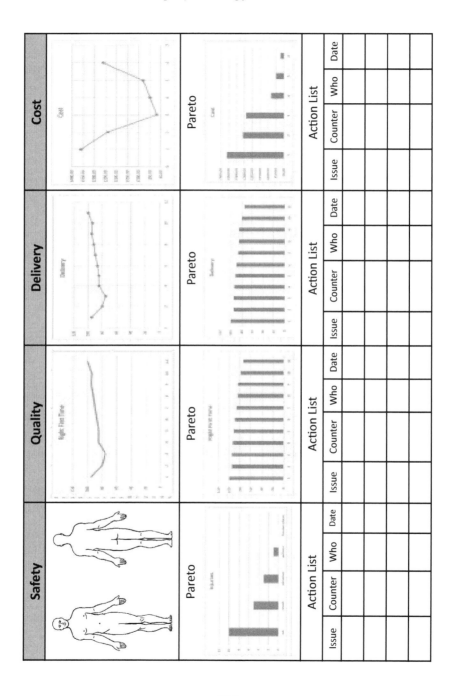

around Brian. "This is an SQDC board; I have put some examples so that you can see how it works. This is about how we measure and track our performance as a team and take action when there is a problem. So, if we start with safety, as you can see there is an outline of a human, we will use this as a measles chart." "Excuse me, what is a measles chart?" asked Derek. "We add little red sticky coloured spots to the outline for the location of the injury. This gives a visual of which part of the body we are seeing the most injuries, so with all of the spots on the chart it looks like it has measles. Hence, this is why it is called a measles chart. This type of chart is not just used for safety but also for issues such as faults on parts. For instance, it can be used for snagging. Does that answer your question?" "Yes, it does thanks." "From that, we need to understand the type of injuries. The ones that I have used here are cuts, abrasions, breaks, splinters and foreign objects, and this last one refers to things like a grinding spark getting into the eye. We collect the data on this and we turn it into a Pareto chart where we can see what the biggest problem is and then we look at taking action to try and prevent this type of injury occurring. The second category is quality; this is where we measure things that are done right first time. So, anything that needs reworking, we capture and put it into a Pareto chart so that we can attack the top issues to prevent them from happening again. Delivery is all about where you are on the project so that we know what is on time and what has fallen back. Again, we create a Pareto chart so that we can take action to deal with the top issues. Finally, we look at the costs. This does not refer to the cost of materials or labour as this is tracked elsewhere. What we are tracking here is the hidden costs that don't normally get captured." "I don't understand how there can be hidden costs, either you pay for something or you don't," observed Pete. Some of the others nodded in agreement with Pete. "Let me explain; Pete, let's suppose that you have run out of cable, so you can't proceed, what would you do?" Pete answered quickly "I would be onto Dave or Mike to get some ordered." "Ok, and after you have ordered it then what?" "I guess I would look around to see if there is anything else that I could be getting on with or help one of the others." "that is fine. However, because you can no longer do the job until you get more cable you are no longer effective on the build so your waiting for cable becomes a cost. For argument sake with labour and overheads, we shall say that the cost for you is seventy pounds an hour, and that you have had to wait for five hours to get your cable, then this is what the hidden cost would be." Brian wrote the figures out on the board so that they could all see.

£70 per hour x 5 hours waiting time = £70 x 5 = £350

£350 = cost to the company

5 hours = delay to the build

"I can see where you are coming from now, it is starting to make sense" said Pete. "This is only a small portion of what we track here. Obviously, we will feed in the data that we have captured from the items that were not done right first time, and things like scrap. Overtime will also come into this; as overtime is used as a catch up because it could not be done in normal time, so it is an extra cost. If drawings get updated, then this is a not right first time in itself and then you have to change things. Therefore, it would be a rework hence again we cost it. Extra inventory is also monitored as we need to have just the right amount. Basically, anything that causes a change, or a delay will be costed. This is why I was saying that I cannot do this by myself. We need to have teamwork as I need each of you to tell us when you have an issue so that we can take early action to prevent it from happening again. This board makes it visible to everyone and we can all to see where the problems are and how we are dealing with it through the countermeasures." Dave was thoughtful, "this makes sense, I have lost money and time in the past I didn't know how no matter how hard I looked, but this simple board and metrics brings it to the surface" he thought. Dave was brought out of his thoughts when he heard Brian mention his name. "Dave will now explain what we are doing on this project." Dave cleared his throat and addressed his team. "We are going to add an extra floor by creating a loft conversion, then we are going to change the building into a six bed HMO, we will also be adding a conservatory as one of the communal rooms. This means we will require a higher standard of work as we not only get visits from the building regulators but also from the environmental officer, and this HMO is aimed at professional people, so it will be high spec with en-suite in each of the rooms." Brian excused himself whilst the team were talking amongst themselves and went back to the office where he took Dave's copy of the drawing off the wall and went back to the canteen. "Give me a hand Dave." Dave helped Brian stick the drawing to the wall next to the SQDC board. "Right; guys, this is what we are building, get acquainted with it." Brian said and stepped away from the drawing to allow the team to gather around and discuss the plan amongst themselves. Twenty minutes later the conversation started to die down, Dave looked at his watch "Ok you lot the first skip will be here in an hour, so let's get moving and as those internal walls are not going to take themselves down." The team smiled as they were used to Dave's dry humour, they donned their hardhats and headed out of the canteen and over to the van to get their tools. Some of the team members took the tools that they would need immediately to work on the house into the building whilst other team members took the rest of the tools and placed them in a secure lockup that was on the side of the cabin. It was not long before the sound of hammering and sawing could be heard coming from the house as work got underway.

Several hours later, Max and Connor quickly followed by Nick and Amanda turned up onsite. Max and Connor were wearing their hardhats and safety shoes. Dave greeted them as they arrived. "Morning, hope you had a pleasant drive, Brian is in the cabin." Dave looked down at Nick and Amanda's footwear and shook his head. "Sorry but I can't let you onsite without the right personal protection safety gear. I can provide you with hardhats and safety glasses, but I don't have spare safety shoes and certainly not for ladies. I suggest that you head into town and see if you can get a pair and then come back here." There was a look of disappointment from them both as they were quite excited now that the project was finally underway. "Ok, I guess it is for our own good as well as site safety, we will see what is available for us and be right back."

Dave nodded in agreement. "See you later." He watched as they headed back to their car, and then he headed over to the office to see Max and Connor. When he walked into the cabin, he saw that Brian was taking Max and Connor through the SQDC board and explaining how it worked. Dave put the kettle on, made them all a drink, and handed them out as Brian finished his explanation. "Well, this is something that we can take away with us for future builds as it makes a lot of sense to track these items. I particularly like the tracking of costs as this is not something that we have thought about before, as the normal thing is that you have a budget and you try to work to it. I never even considered that there could be hidden costs." "If it makes you feel better Max, I didn't consider these costs either, and I am more astute than you." The other chuckled at Dave quip. "Max tells me that Nick and Amanda are here" Brian asked Dave. "They were but I had to send them away as they did not have safety shoes, so they have gone into town to see if they can get a pair." "Fair enough Dave, I agree. No one should be onsite without the proper safety gear, no matter who they are. You can take Max and Connor and introduce them to the team and they can see the progress so far, and I will wait for Nick and Amanda."

Brian busied himself going over the plans as he waited. Ten minutes later, he looked up from his desk and through the window and he could see Nick's car pull up outside. He got up and went to out to greet them. As he approached them he could see not only had they purchased safety shoes but hardhats too. "I see that you are prepared this time" Brian said as he shook hands with Nick and kissed Amanda's cheek. "Well after Dave wouldn't let us onsite we thought that we may as well get all our own gear as we no doubt will need them in the future, so we also got hardhats and safety glasses." "Good for you, after this project has finished you will have picked up a lot of useful information and experience that will make subsequent projects a lot easier. Right, lets head to the cabin first and then introduce you to Dave's team." Brian led the way, took them to the cabin, and showed them around. Once he had given them the tour, he then explained the SQDC board to them, which they found fascinating. Brian then took them over to the building and introduced them to the rest of the team. They looked around and saw that some of the internal walls had already been taken down and the rubble was being wielded out on wheelbarrows to the skip that had been delivered onsite earlier. "I'm surprised at the progress, it has gone a lot faster than I had expected," Nick observed. "I have a good bunch of lads, who know what is expected of them, so they just get on with it" Dave said with a hint of pride. "When will you need material onsite?" Brian asked. Dave rubbed his chin as he thought what still needed to be done to basically create an empty box. "I think that we would need to have it for two days' time." "What material do you need first?" Dave looked at Brian with a puzzled look on his face "just deliver it and we can sort out from there." "Sorry Dave but we are not going to do that; we are going to employ JIT." "What is JIT when it's at home?" Dave asked. "JIT is short for just in time, which is a method in that the only materials that are currently being used are onsite. This way we keep a low inventory, which in turn means that we will not need a large storage area. This also saves us in costs as there is less time off the job with the trades looking for the right material that they need for the job." "But how does it work?" Dave asked. "Essentially it is a pull system, in that we will order as we need it and just before we run out of material. For instance, we will need timber to produce stud walls and the loft conversion. We have already decided that we will start with the loft first, so we order the timber for the roof joists and nothing else. You will have estimated the timber that we will require for the joists so that is what we order, we will put a signal before the last of the timber to inform us that we need to either order some more because we have under estimated or that we have sufficient timber to finish the job so that we can order the next set of materials such as flooring for the loft, and so on." Nick and Amanda watched as they waited for Dave to make a comment. "I have never come across this before and I'm not sure about it. However, I will give it a go seeing as up to now your methods have worked." "Thanks Dave, I really appreciate it that you are willing to listen and have a go, which as my coach and mentor Trevor will tell you very few people will, as they are stuck in the if it isn't broke don't fix it attitude." Dave nodded "I would like to meet this coach of yours as he sounds interesting if he has taught you all of these things." "I will happily introduce you to him, as he has said he will come here onsite at some point during this project." "You will like him Dave; he has really helped us when we went through a bit of a low period recently" Amanda added. Dave nodded and then became all business again "So what is this signal that we will be using to get more material?" he asked. "Let's head back over to the office and I will show you."

They were sat in the office and Brain took opened his laptop, which was attached to a large monitor giving him two screens to work on, he then opened a document, placed it on the monitor screen, and started to create a signal card. The others watched as he worked and ten minutes later, he had finished.

ORDER NOW					
Part Description			**Part No**		
Quantity		**Lead Time**		**Order Date**	
Supplier				**Due Date**	
Contact			**Ordered By**		
Required		**Not Required**		**Order Next Material**	
ORDER NOW					

"Well this is what it looks like, it is pretty much self-explanatory, but I will populate it for you just to show you what a completed card looks like." Brian tapped away at his keyboard and populated the signal card.

ORDER NOW					
Part Description			**Part No**		
4" thick x 6" wide x 12' long pine timber			4612PN		
Quantity	20	**Lead Time**	1 Week	**Order Date**	21/7/16
Supplier	ACE Timber Merchants			**Due Date**	28/7/16
Contact	A Nother		**Ordered By**	Brian	
Required		**Not Re-quired**		**Order Next Material**	
ORDER NOW					

"The card will be pre-populated by us and placed with the materials; in this case for instance we could fix it to the fifteenth piece of timber in the stack. When the guys get to this piece of timber it can be decided if more is required then they will tick the required box and enter the quantity, in this example it's twenty, if they do not require it then they will tick both the not required box and order next material box. This card is then handed into the office where we will process it." "Well, it looks simple enough and the amount of paperwork that my guys have to do to order material is minimalist as all they need at the most is a couple of ticks and a quantity which is good, and we will all know we have to order otherwise we will run out of material and the job comes to a stop." "That is the whole idea with this pull system, which is why it is useful to implement." "Why is it called a pull system? Dave asked. "It's called that because we allow the work to pull what it needs so it limits the amount of work in process, so the job has to be finished before moving on to the next one. "Brian turned to Nick and Amanda "You can use this in your business too for you and your employees to order things like copier paper, envelopes, ink cartridges etc. this is what I do in my own business, you just need to adjust the signal card slightly as you do not need the bottom line as you will be ordering the same material and quantity all of the time based on your normal usage. So, yours will look something like this." Brian then made the changes to the signal card and populated it for office material.

ORDER NOW					
Part Description			**Part No**		
500 x 80 gsm photocopier paper			PCP80		
Quantity	20	**Lead Time**	1 Day	**Order Date**	21/7/16
Supplier	ACE Office Supplies			**Due Date**	28/7/16
Contact	A Nother		**Ordered By**	Amanda	
ORDER NOW					

"There you go; there is the office version for you. You simply put this in between your packs of photocopier paper and when this card is exposed you simply order some more and in the same quantity." "What a great idea, I always seem to forget to order more and have to run out and get some" replied Nick. "You mean that you run out and I go out and get more" Amanda corrected. Nick looked a bit sheepish, "Ok dear, point taken." Brian and Dave smiled at Nick, which made him turn slightly red in the cheeks "I guess I have just been put in my place" he chuckled. Amanda was looking thoughtful, "I have seen something like this when I have been shopping at the supermarket" she said. "You are a bang on, Amanda; this idea was taken from the US supermarkets when some Toyota engineers were on a visit there in the late nineteen forties, they observed how it worked and introduced into manufacturing, they called it Kanban which in Japanese means visual signal." Amanda was pleased that she was right in recognising a similar system. "Ok history lesson over, I will print this off Dave so that you can explain it to your team. If they have any questions that you can't answer let me know and I will answer them." Brian printed off half a dozen copies and Dave retrieved them from the printer and went off to talk to his team.

"I want you both to be onsite on a regular basis, as I need you to understand how things are done and for you to have an understanding of the build. In this way, you will be able to manage small projects in the future and know what you are dealing with. You are going to be making a lot of observations as we will be going on lots of Gemba walks." Nick and Amanda looked puzzled, and then Nick spoke up "Excuse me Brian, but what is a Gemba walk?" he asked. "Ah yes sorry, in my business we do this so regularly that it has become part of the normal language. Hence, I automatically said it as if you understood what I was talking about, which you obviously don't so let me explain. Gemba is a Japanese term meaning to go where the work is done, in other words the pulse of your business. In the case of this project, it means where the actual refurbishment is taking place, so it is in the building not in this office. When we go into the building, we are looking at flow as we did in the spaghetti diagram that we did so that we can shorten times, therefore we need to constantly monitor it. This cannot be done from an office, as you will be assuming what is happening, this is a case of putting boots on the ground and seeing with your own eyes what is actually happening. If we see a problem we don't just dive in there and try to put it right, we involve the people and ask the question why it was done in this way, as there may be another issue that we are not aware of which we may have to fix first. By involving people, we are coaching them so that we can start to change the culture from blame to an open one where we can improve critical thinking skills that can be used to identify waste in the system, as in the acronym TIM WOOD that we have talked about, and to use problem-solving skills. When we go on a Gemba walk we need to be unassuming; we need to listen more than we talk, and we need to build up a relationship of trust." "Well, that sounds fairly easy, so we should be able to manage that" replied Nick. Brian shook his head, "Sorry Nick but you are wrong. Although on the surface it seems simple enough, this is not an easy thing to do. First of all, you need to be able to stand quietly and observe. At first people will be wary of you, as they do not like being watched so you have to put them at ease. Then you need to understand what you are looking for, which in some cases it will be easy, as it will stand out like a sore thumb. However, in other cases the issue may be so subtle that you will miss it. This is why Gemba walks will require patience and lots of practice." "I can understand it on a project like this, but how do you do this in our business?" Amanda asked. "We apply exactly the same method; the only difference is in the pulse of your business. For instance, if you are doing your book keeping then at that moment in time that would be your business pulse. So, Nick would be the fresh pair of eyes that would observe you and see if there is any waste or issues in the work that you are doing. Does that answer your question?" Brian asked. "Thank you, it does, I now see where you are coming from with this." "Good, so let's get some practice in, so we shall now go observe some of Dave's team at work. There are some note pads over on my desk, so help yourself and let's get going." Amanda went and got them a pad each and they followed Brian out to the building and they went inside and found a spot where they could observe whilst not interfering with the work that was going on. At first, Pete who was working on the electrics looked up and momentarily stopped working as he sensed he was being watched, so Brian decided that this was a good time to talk to him. "Hi Pete, sorry if we have put you off your work we didn't want to disturb you whilst you were working especially as you are dealing with electrics." Pete relaxed "No problem, how can I help?" he asked. "If you don't mind we just want to observe how you do your job so we can get a feel for it." Pete was immediately on his guard "What exactly are you trying to do?" he asked. "Don't worry it is nothing cynical such as time and motion studies. What we are looking for is continuous improvements such as removing unnecessary waste and obstacles from what you are doing to make your job easier." "What do you mean by waste?" Pete asked still not convinced. Brian went on to explain the acronym TIM WOOD and how it would help the project if they could remove as much waste as possible, as it would also have helped with gaining them their bonus. Pete physically relaxed he had not realised until that point that he had been tense "Thanks for explaining to me, I can see where you are coming from and you are right. There may be some things that I am not aware of and just accept, which could be termed as waste." "Thank you for your cooperation it is much appreciated and as the subject matter expert if we spot something we will certainly consult with you to get your opinion and find a solution." Pete had never been called a subject matter expert before and he decided that it had a nice ring to it. "You carry on and observe all you want" he said and with a huge grin he took out his screwdriver from his overall leg pocket and continued with the work he was doing. Brian, Nick and Amanda continued watching Pete as he worked. Pete was rummaging around in his toolbox for several minutes before finding the tie wrap he was looking for. "What did you just see?" Brian asked Nick and Amanda. Nick replied without hesitation "Pete just getting stuff out of his toolbox." "What about you Amanda?" "Pete was just rummaging around for a plastic strap. Have we missed something?" she asked. "I saw waste." Nick and Amanda looked quizzically at Brian, but he remained silent, as he wanted them to think about it. Nick went through the seven wastes in his mind "Transport, Inventory, Motion, Waiting, Over Producing, Over Processing, Defects" but he could not see where in this list did Pete going through his toolbox fitted in. Amanda was going through the same list in her mind and eliminated all but one that she thought was a possibility. "Motion," she said. "But he didn't go anywhere" Nick pointed out. "Please explain Amanda" Brian said. "Well, I think it is motion because although he did not go anywhere as Nick has pointed out, he did waste time looking through his toolbox and taking things out and putting things back, which is a form of motion." Brian smiled "You are correct Amanda." Amanda was pleased with herself as she viewed this as a test that she had to pass." Now keep observing and see if you can spot anything else that may be an issue." They carried on watching for another hour but at this stage could see no more issues. "Well I'm glad that we don't have to watch anymore, it becomes boring" said Nick as he glanced at his watch. "You have got off light Nick. If you were working for Taiichi Ohno at Toyota, he would have taken you to the shop floor, drawn a circle and asked you to step into the circle. You would have been left there to make observations and come up with recommendations. He would then come over to you after several hours and ask what you had observed and if he didn't like your responses you would remain in the circle and again told to make observations and you could be there for eight hours or more." "Bloody hell that sounds horrendous, I'm sure that not many people stayed on after that." "You are wrong Nick, the people who were subjected to this considered it an honour because they were learning from a great master and many of them went on to be great engineers and managers within the company." Nick shook his head "I wouldn't put up with it no matter how much I would learn from him." "That is because of your modern western thinking, had you been brought up in the East then you would accept it as it is part of your apprenticeship." "I guess. Right, what do we do now?" "We will look at ways to help Pete so that he doesn't have to take half of the contents of his toolbox out before he finds what he was looking for." Pete by this time had gathered up his tools and headed over to Brian, Nick and Amanda. "Well guys did you spot anything that I should be aware of?" he asked. "Actually, Pete we did, and we will need your help to fix it." Pete was now intrigued, "What did you see?" he asked eagerly. "We noticed that you had to rummage around to get a cable tie from your toolbox." "Is that it?" Pete asked incredulously as he was expecting a lot more. Brian smiled as he had come across situations like this on many occasions. "Let me explain why it is so important." Brian turned his pad to a clean page and began to write as he explained. "You took ten minutes to find your cable tie, now if we divide ten minutes by sixty, as there are sixty minutes in an hour we get point one six six, now if we multiply it by our overhead cost of say seventy pounds per hour we get eleven pounds and sixty-six pence which is the cost of those ten minutes."

10 minutes / 60 minutes = 0.166-hour   0.166-hour X £70 = £11.66

"Now, let's say that on average this happens every hour on an eight-hour shift. Therefore, we multiply eleven pounds and sixty-six pence by eight we end up with a figure of ninety-three pounds and twenty-eight pence."

£11.66 X 8 hours = £93.28

"If we then multiply this figure by five days a week that you work on this build we get four hundred and sixty-six pounds and forty pence."

£93.28 X 5 days = £466.40

"Let's say that the build takes twelve weeks. If we now multiply the ninety-three pounds and twenty-eight pence by twelve we get five thousand five hundred and ninety-six pounds and eighty pence, which you can see is a huge cost to the build."

£466.40 X 12 weeks = £5596.80

"That is the cost; now let's look at the hours. Ten minutes multiplied by eight, which is the one an hour average over the eight-hour shift, we get eighty minutes"

10 minutes X 8 = 80 minutes

"Now we can multiply these eighty minutes by our five-day week and now we have four hundred minutes."

80 minutes X 5 days = 400 minutes

"We now multiply our four hundred minutes by our twelve weeks and we get four thousand eight hundred minutes."

400 minutes X 12 weeks = 4800 minutes

"If we now convert these minutes to hours by dividing them by sixty we get eighty hours."

4800 minutes / 60 minutes = 80 hours

"If we now divide the hours by your eight hours shift it gives us ten days. This is the amount of time we lose on the project."

80 hours / 8 hours = 10 days

Pete let out a low whistle "Wow, when you put it like that I can understand your concern." Pete shook his head as he took it in. "I would never have thought that such an insignificant delay could cause a significant cost in time and money." Brian tapped him on the shoulder in sympathy "You are not the only one who has had this thought, and you certainly won't be the last. I too have been caught out in the same way as you by my coach and friend Trevor when he looked into my business. He really opened my eyes as I too was throwing away money and time. The trick now is to understand what we are going to do to solve the problem." Nick kept thinking about the money they would save if they could solve the problem. Whilst Amanda was thinking not of the money but the amount of time that could potentially be saved, this would mean they could get their tenants in quicker and therefore start earning from the property. "The problem is obviously my toolbox and how it is organised." "I would agree with you on that Pete" replied Brian. "I may have to buy a new toolbox to get in everything I need in an organised manner." "Before you think about buying a toolbox that you may have to modify, why not come up with a design and we can see if we can get Joe to build you a prototype out of wood, and once you are happy with it we could possibly get something made." Pete was thoughtful and slowly nodded his head "I think that I could do that."

"Once you have a design in mind we can get Max to draw it up for you, so that Joe has a set of drawings that he can work to." "Won't that mean a cost in their time and money?" Pete asked. Brian was amused that Pete was now thinking in this way. "Yes, there will be a short-term cost, but it will be less than the long-term cost, so we should do it." Pete looked relieved "Ok boss, I will get on with it." It was not lost on Brian that he had been called boss by Pete; he knew from this simple sentence that he had been accepted by Pete as part of his team. "Great, I will look forward to seeing your design." Pete strolled off with a smile on his face and a step in his stride. "Well, he seems happy enough" Nick observed. "Yes, he does, and more importantly he understands what we are trying to do so he will explain it to the others so there will be less resistance to being observed and to change." The three of them went back across to the office where they met up with Dave, Max and Connor. "How do you think we are doing Dave?" Brian asked. "I think that we will need our first set of materials for the day after tomorrow." "Great, let's get on to the suppliers and make sure that they deliver exactly on time." Dave pulled out the scheme of works and went over the list of materials with Nick. Fifteen minutes later Nick was on the phone with the suppliers placing his orders and reiterating with them the importance of having the material delivered on time. Brian and the others were quite amused to hear Nick tell each of them that if it wasn't delivered on time, him and the supplier will become the best of friends because he would be placed on speed dial and will be called every five minutes until his material was onsite.

Pete was sat in the canteen with the rest of the team but instead of joining in with the rest of the conversation, he had a sheet of paper in front of him and was deep in thought. "What are you doing Pete?" asked Derek. "I'm thinking." "As that is a first for you Pete, you mind that you don't hurt yourself" Joe quipped in friendly banter. The others laughed; Pete smiled and went back to thinking. The others realised that Pete was quite serious with whatever he was thinking about. Mike was concerned "What is it Pete, is it anything that we can help with?" he asked. Pete looked around at the team and then started to explain what Brian had spotted and the figures that he had been shown and how he was now trying to come up with a design for a toolbox. The team were fascinated by what they had been told and now understood why Brian and the owners were standing quietly in one spot watching. Derek took out his phone and using the calculator app, went over the figures and announced that it was correct. Each of the team began to wonder if they too were doing things that would cost the project and could ultimately affect their bonus. "Right, let's brainstorm this baby. I'm sure that between us we can come up with a toolbox design that will help you Pete" suggested Mike. The rest of the team agreed it would be a good idea, so Mike went over to the office to find a large piece of paper. "Sorry to interrupt, have you got a large sheet of paper that I could have?" Mike asked. "I have some paper that you can have Mike." Max went over to his bag to get some paper. "What do you need it for Mike?" Dave asked. "We are going to brainstorm a toolbox design for Pete." "You are going to do what?" Dave repeated not quite believing what he had heard. Before Mike could answer, Brian answered the question for him. "It is a project that I have set for Pete based on our observation." Brian went on to explain what they had seen and showed them the numbers from his note book. When he had finished, the others were flabbergasted by the numbers. Dave rubbed his chin then addressed Mike "Joe is going to be too busy with the project to be making a toolbox, but you were asking a few weeks ago about taking on your lad as an apprentice carpenter. At the time I said no as I could not afford to take him on. Well, if Max and Connor agree I think that we can offer him a job as no doubt we shall be seeing a few more small off build projects that he could do under Joe's supervision." Dave looked at his partners "I have no problem taking on an apprentice if it will help us both now and in the future" Max said. "I concur, besides we could do with more young blood around here, as I am beginning to feel like a kid around you lot" Connor joked. Max regarded his son "With comments like that you will be on the naughty step." The others grinned. "Ok Mike that's settled, bring your lad onsite tomorrow so he can get started and in the meantime sort out which college course he will need and get him enrolled." "Thanks boss, he will be a happy bunny when I tell him the news." "Well, what are you waiting for, get your paper and get on with it." Although it sounded like a dismissal from Dave, Mike knew that Dave deep down was quite considerate and would help where he could, he just didn't like to show it. Hence, to people who did not know him he seemed quiet and sounded abrupt when he spoke as it was usually in short sentences to and to the point. Mike collected the paper that Max gave him and with a big smile went back to the team.

"Brian are you not going to supervise the team with their design?" asked Connor. "No, at this moment in time I think that they can work on this on their own as they will form their own quality circle." Now the others were intrigued, and Max was the first to ask "What is a quality circle?" Brian smiled, "History lesson time. Quality circles started in Japan and were developed by Kaoru Ishikawa." "Is that the same Ishikawa that created the fish bone diagram?" asked Amanda. "Yes, it is Amanda. The quality circle is a method of getting a small group of people who do similar work to work together to solve or improve a local issue. They are normally led by a supervisor and when they have a solution, they will present it to the management. The management will then check the analysis and the proposed solution and if they are happy they will give the go ahead and the group will implement it. Ishikawa worked with the Japanese Union of Scientists and Engineers known as JUSE to coordinate the movement across Japan and was very successful. Manufacturers in the West saw these quality circles, decided it was the secret to Japanese success, and so tried to implement it in their businesses but it failed, as they did not grasp it properly. You see, in order for quality circles to work the workers must be given time to meet and come up with solutions. Management must not interfere by telling them what needs to be sorted and what the solutions are expected to be put in place. This is the part that the West did not do effectively as they tended to dictate what they wanted the quality circle to look at; they did not give them time to meet as they saw it was a loss of time in production and as usual with management, they had already decided what the solutions were even though they did not go anywhere near the job. So, in effect the quality circles in general in the West were set up to fail." "So, do you think that the team will become a quality circle?" Max asked. "I think with a little bit of encouragement and guidance they will run their own circle, which of course will be of benefit to your company as they will start to find and iron out issues which will make you more efficient and effective." They could hear the team at work next door as suggestions were being shouted out for the toolbox design and they sounded like they were having fun doing it.

Several Days later, Pete's new toolbox was ready for trial. Pete inspected the quality of the work before telling Mike's son Steve that it would suffice. Joe was immediately on his case telling him that the lad had done a really good job on it and if he did not appreciate the work of his apprentice, he could go and find someone else to make him a toolbox. Pete held up his hands in surrender, he knew that Joe had taken a shine to Steve as he had a good instinctive feel for working with wood, which is why Pete had ribbed him for the quality of the work. Pete took his new toolbox and began to transfer all his tools to it; it did look elegant and functional. As soon as he appeared with it the other team members stood and gave him a round of applause. "Now you have no excuses, so now you will have to make up the time you have already lost us" Derek shouted. "I already work faster than you lot" Pete retorted. "Yes, but you have to keep going back to it because your quality does not match your speed" Jeff replied. There were more laughter and mickey taking before the team settled down and got back to work. Brian, Nick and Amanda found a spot where they could have uninterrupted views of Pete working and began to observe him. Pete became aware of them, but he took no noticed as he got on with his work. Over the last few days the whole team had got used to seeing the three of them standing and watching them work. Pete found the new toolbox worked well for him, as everything was organised and labelled, and he could pick up tools and parts quickly and easily without having to look for them. So, as far as he was concerned it was a great success. An hour later Mike wandered over to the three of them "Well boss, is it an improvement or not?" he asked. He stood waiting for the reply as Brian thumbed through his notes. "I can honestly say that the toolbox works beautifully, we have not seen Pete rummaging around in the box at all, so well done to you and the rest of the team for coming up with the design" Brian smiled. "Well it is a good job that it works because now we are going to be busy designing more custom toolboxes as everyone wants a bespoke toolbox that suits their needs, and before you ask that also includes me." Brian grinned, "That Mike is usually the way, but at least it is a positive move and of course your lad Steve will gain from the experience." "That he will, and of course we will cut down our time and costs." Nick shook his head, "I have never heard a builder yet worry about going over time and budget, this must be a first." Mike smiled at Nick's good-humoured remark "That's because normally there is no incentives, so builders may bid for two or three jobs and spend a little bit of time on each site. Dave is one of the few that does not work that way, as he prefers one job at a time and done correctly so we don't have to come back once we have packed up. The main difference with this job is that if we fail to come in on budget and on time we get hit in our pockets. But if we do manage to do it for under then we get an extra bonus, so it is pretty fair all round, and the lads are looking forward to receiving their pay out." Nick chuckled "Are you so sure that is going to happen?" he asked. "We are certain of it, especially as you are also helping us become more efficient with your Gemba walks," Mike winked at him as he said it. Nick hadn't thought about that, but it was true what Mike had said. He has been unwittingly helping the team achieve their goal. Amanda laughed "He's got you there Nick, and you keep telling me that you're the clever one" she joked. They all laughed at the look on Nick's face that sort of said he had been conned.

They had been on the project for several weeks and everything went well and mainly to plan. There had been only one hiccup with a supplier who did not deliver on time; if he thought that Nick was joking when he had told him that he was now on speed dial and they would become the best of friends until he got his delivery he soon found that Nick was true to his word, as he rang him every five minutes and warned him that if he hung up on him or did not take his call he would be camped out in his office. After the first few calls, the supplier knew that Nick meant it. Therefore, he diverted a lorry that was supposed to go to a major developer to deliver Nick's materials, as it would be less painful, as he knew that developers always expected some delays, as this was normal for a project. After that incident the supplier never failed to deliver on time and always made sure that the quality was up to scratch as he had a feeling he would never hear the last of it if he delivered anything remotely substandard. The team was getting close to the point where they would need to know the layout for the kitchen and bathroom so that the electrics and plumbing could be put in. Amanda was working with Connor trying to figure it out. The only problem was that each had their own ideas and instead of compromise, they were being stubborn about it. Brian walked in on them when the discussion was getting a bit heated as Amanda was looking at the aesthetics of the layout whilst Connor was looking at practicalities. "Ok guys, I think that you two need to have a break before things get really out of hand. Trevor is coming onsite today to have a look around and as you two can't compromise or listen to reason, I'm going to ask him to make judgement based on what you tell him." "He is not an architect so why should he make judgement?" Connor asked. His lips were tight as he tried to control his anger at the suggestion of having a stranger look at his work. "Trevor is a very knowledgeable person, who will look at things from what the evidence tells him, so he will not get emotional about it, currently he has been hired as a consultant by Dalton Towers, so I think he knows a thing or two about the construction industry." Brian looked at Connor as he made his point. Although Connor knew about Dalton Towers and its reputation in the construction business he was not about to let go so easily, but just as he was about to become vocal Amanda spoke up. "I will go with Trevor's decision." Brian nodded "Thank you Amanda." Connor was not expecting Amanda to give in so easily especially the way that she held her ground with him. So, he suddenly found himself out on a limb and did not help that both Brian and Amanda were staring at him waiting for a reply. Connor took a deep breath "Ok, I will go with what your man says." "Thank you, Connor." Brian left the two of them in the office and went off to see Dave to let him know that Trevor would be visiting.

Forty-five minutes later Trevor arrived onsite as Brian went to greet him, Dave noted with satisfaction that Trevor was wearing the correct safety equipment. Brian introduced Trevor to Dave, they shook hands and Trevor asked if they could go for a tour of the project. Brian excused himself and headed to the office as Trevor and Dave went into the building. "So how are you finding this project so far?" Trevor asked. Dave took a moment to gather his thoughts before answering. "I must admit that at first I was a bit dubious of all of the things that Brian had us doing from the start, but when I thought about it they made a lot of sense, so I have got to the point where I will try it first before passing judgement." "Good to see someone that has some common sense, often I have to argue and fight for things to get done, and then it is with reluctance until they can see the benefits. Therefore, your words are refreshing. Now let me ask you what benefits you have seen from this project?" Dave rubbed his chin, "My team are all fired up looking for ways to improve; it has now become a competition to find out who is causing a delay and how it can be fixed. Materials are easy to find onsite as we do not have it all over the place as they arrive just in time, we all check the SQDC board at our metrics and we know where we are with everything. Most importantly, so far, we are under budget and under time. Therefore, all the things that we have learnt so far has been of great benefit." Trevor smiled, "I am glad to hear it, now tell me about yourself." Dave hesitated, as he hated talking about himself. Hence, he started to give Trevor a summary, but Trevor asked him some poignant questions and before he knew it, he was talking to Trevor quite openly. Trevor also explained to Dave about his own background, which Dave was quite impressed with, which spoke volumes as Dave was not easily impressed. Soon, the pair were talking like long lost friends as they toured the building. Trevor was introduced to the individual team members as they toured around and was shown some of the ideas that the team had implemented including the customised toolboxes. Trevor had a brief chat with everyone, asked them questions about the project, and was happy with the answers that he had received. "You have a good team Dave; just make sure that you look after them." Dave smiled at the praise his team had received. "Don't worry, I will." "You also need to challenge them." Dave frowned. "What do you mean?" he asked. "At the moment the team are on a high because they have been given lots of small challenges to think about as they work on this project, but it will get to a point that they will relax and that is when small corners start to get cut. To prevent that from happening keep giving them challenges and stretched goals, that way they will start to reach their own potential and you will have a created a culture of teamwork and problem solving." Dave was quite for a few minutes as he stroked his chin and went over in his mind what Trevor had said. Trevor watched and stayed quiet; he knew that Dave had to think about this before he could accept it as being true; it was a turning moment that he had no intention of interrupting it. "Thinking back to my days in the RAF, we had lots of challenges that kept us on our toes and made us think, and this really is no different, so you are right; I do need to look after my team by constantly challenging them. Thank you for bringing it to my attention." Trevor nodded. "Dave you have good leadership skills, so I know that your team will be in good capable hands. Right, let's see what is going on in the office."

They walked in to the office and Trevor was greeted warmly by Nick and Amanda. Connor noticed this and was not pleased, as he believed that as Trevor knew the owners he would be more likely to be in their favour when it came to decisions. Trevor was then introduced to Max and Connor, he found Max open and friendly whereas he saw there was tension in Connor and was greeted coldly by him. *There was something amiss here*, he thought as he glanced around at the others and that is when he noticed Amanda staring at Connor with tight lips. He decided that before they continued to discuss the project he needed to find out what was going on. "Amanda, Connor I would like to discuss the project with you two first." Brian was not surprised that Trevor had picked up the tension between these two and knowing Trevor as he did, he knew that he would address it immediately. "Max, Dave, let's go see how the team is doing." Brian closed the office door behind him and led them away. Trevor stood in front of Amanda and Connor, looked at them, and in a low calm voice asked "Ok, who is going to tell me what is going on between you two?" There was an awkward silence for a minute then Amanda spoke. "We have been looking at the layout of the kitchen and bathrooms and we just can't agree on it at the moment." Trevor looked at Connor, "Care to expand on that?" Before Connor could gather his thoughts, his anger was suddenly unleashed. "I'm the architect, I know what I am doing to maximise the space, not make it look pretty so I do not need amateurs telling me what to do or how to do it." Connor looked defiantly at Trevor. "Please be seated" Trevor indicated the chairs to Amanda and Connor. Amanda sat down and waited whilst Connor remained standing for a short while in defiance, but Trevor calmly stood staring at him until with reluctance Connor sat. "I think the pair of you have let your emotions rule your head and you need to learn to work with each other." Trevor turned to Amanda "First of all you need to listen to Connor when it comes to trying to maximise the layout to reach its full potential." Trevor glanced at Connor who had a look of triumph on his face. "And you Connor need to learn to listen to your client because at the end of the day they pay your wages." Connor suddenly didn't feel so comfortable as he knew that Trevor was right. "You two need to be able to see things from each other's perspective." Connor suddenly interrupted "How can we do that?" "If you will let me finish that is what I was just about to explain to you." Connor squirmed under Trevor's gaze; he took a deep breath and nodded. When Trevor was satisfied that he would not be interrupted he continued. "There is a method called three Ps, which stand for Preparation, Production, and Process. This is a method that comes from manufacturing that is used to design layouts of the factory ready to introduce a new product line, which is basically what we have here with this project." Amanda raised her hand to speak "Yes Amanda." "I don't understand; how can a building relate to a factory?" Connor wanted to know the answer to that question too, so he was glad that Amanda asked it. Trevor smiled, "The similarities are more than you think. When a factory wants to introduce a new product line it has to be planned so that it will cause the least interruption to the existing manufacturing, it has to be up, and running without any snags as any delay will cost the company in time and money. With a build you are changing the layout. So, in effect, that is your new product line, and you want it in without any problems because the delay will cost you time and money." Amanda and Connor nodded in agreement, as they could understand what Trevor was saying and relating it to the project. "In order to see how the layout will work we will have to try both your ways" Connor suddenly stood up "That would mean extra work as we would have to move pipes and electrics just to try both methods that is stupid." Trevor remained calm and indicated that Connor should sit down. Connor reluctantly did so but was not happy about what he had heard. "You must learn patience Connor" Trevor admonished. "What the factory do is to get a cross functional team to build a model of the factory and play around with the different layouts, once they are happy they will then build a full-size mock-up to see what it looks like and to see if there are any problems that show up. Instead of building a model we will build a mock-up of the kitchen and en-suite bathrooms from wood and cardboard and try them directly to see if the layout works, and once we are happy it becomes set in stone and we do not change it." Trevor looked at the pair of them and there was a reluctant nod from Connor. "Do you still have an issue with it?" Trevor asked. "I am just thinking that we just may be wasting time." "Not really, by doing it this way we can actually save a lot of work, say for instance we build it to your design theory and we find that a cupboard door impedes on something, so then that means it comes up a snag on the snagging list and someone has to try and figure out a solution. Whereas if we produce the mock-up with opening doors, draws etc. then we can see what it will look like and know what to change before we have the expense of putting in the actual units, so it means we can fit it and forget it as we know there will be no problems with it." Connor thought about it and realised what Trevor was saying made sense and it would also prove one way or another who was right. "Ok, I understand now." "Good, so now I want you two to work together with Steve to build the mock-ups and to try the layouts." Trevor saw that the pair of them were happier with the compromise that he had suggested as now they could experiment to their hearts content until the layout was set. He knew that by working together, they would get over their differences because; instead of seeing things on paper in effect they would be seeing what the layout is like in 3D. Trevor was also aware that up until now he was being seen by Connor as the enemy, so he decided it was a good time to stroke his ego a little. "From what I have seen from walking around with Dave, the design that you have come up with, looks really good, I am looking forward to seeing the finished article." Connor beamed at the praise that he was given. "Thank you, I have tried my best." Amanda nodded in agreement "So far it does look good" she admitted. Connor saw that Amanda was genuine in her praise. Connor suddenly went from someone full of pride to being humble. "Thank you, Amanda, as you are the client that means a lot to me." Trevor could see that although Connor was headstrong he really did want to do his best and produce designs that any owner could be proud of. "Connor, would you mind asking the others to come and join us, please?" Connor got up and went off to find Brian, Max and Dave. "How are you finding things Amanda?" "I have learnt a lot. Since your last visit I am now much happier with the business, I can see potential for and dare I say it growth." "That is good, you certainly look a lot happier and you have gained a lot more confidence, especially when it comes to standing your ground." They both smiled at the inference to Amanda's run in with Connor over the layout. "What do you think that you require to be able to grow?" Amanda thought about it for a moment "As we have learnt a lot about our business from you and Brian and we are learning a lot about the actual build, I think that we could expand the portfolio fairly quickly, but there is a limit to how much we can borrow from the banks, so I think that we need a cash injection from potential investors, so that we can give them a good interest return on their money or they can come in with us and share on the cash flow and equity." "So, what do you need to do to get a good investor on board?" "That is the hardest bit, which I haven't figured out yet." Trevor looked at her "Let me ask you a question, how do you make friends with someone?" Amanda thought about the question for a moment before answering "I guess, I start by talking to them, then bit by bit start to get to know them until we get to the point we see each other or keep in contact on a regular basis. Then we start to build up trust and begin to confide in each other." Trevor nodded and smiled. Then it suddenly hit Amanda "I get it, I know what you're trying to say to me, that I should build up a relationship with an investor in the same way that I build up a relationship when I am making friends with someone." "Correct.

The trouble with people is when they want an investor they are just thinking on how to obtain the money, so their approach is to show someone a set of figures and hope that they see it as a good investment, so it is a pretty cold approach. Whereas, if they took time to build the relationship and trust, then the investment will be about the person and not just a set of figures, therefore you will obtain a long-term investor who can help you with several projects, so the portfolio will possibly grow from residential to commercial and from a million to a multimillion pound business." Amanda was excited as she could see what Trevor was telling rang true; she couldn't wait to tell Nick about it so that they could change their approach to try and get an investor on board.

There was a knock at the door and then it opened, and Brian poked his head around. "You ready for us Trevor?" he asked. "Yes, we will join you and you can take me through your SQDC board." Trevor and Amanda went through and joined the others as they gathered around the board and Brian started to take them through it. "One moment Brian" Trevor interrupted. "Connor, can you take us through the board please." Brian smiled as he had been through this exercise with Trevor before in his own organisation. Trevor wanted to make sure that everyone understood the board, so he would pick on someone who was not the leader to talk through it as a test that it was understood. Connor stood in front of the board and to his credit, he spoke with confidence and explained what was happening in each section and how it was being measured. However, Trevor decided that he was going to test the team a bit more before he was satisfied that they understood it. "Can you get the rest of the team here please?" Dave obliged and went off to get the rest of his crew. A few minutes later, they were all gathered around the board. Trevor turned to Derek who happened to be near him. "Can you explain what a Pareto is please?" Derek suddenly felt uncomfortable as everyone turned to him and waited for him to answer. "Take your time and gather your thoughts" Trevor encouraged. Derek took a few deep breaths and then answered, "It is a way of measuring things that could either be an issue because it is wrong or the opposite; that is, a measure where your greatest benefits are coming from." Trevor nodded and then asked Joe "Can you expand on that?" Now it was Joe's turn to take a deep breath "It is known as the eighty twenty rule." "Yes" Trevor encouraged. "Well, it could mean that eighty percent of problems are caused by twenty percent of the issues, so by creating a chart we can see which are the biggest issues, so that we can address them one by one." Trevor nodded "You are on the right lines but is just seeing our biggest issue on a chart enough?" he asked. Apart from Brian who knew from experience what Trevor was, driving at the others looked confused. Mike spoke up "We take the biggest issue and fix it." The others nodded in agreement. "What within that issue will you fix?" Trevor asked. The team were even more confused as they did not know how to answer this, so after several minutes of silence Trevor decided to put them out of their misery. "Say for example that the Pareto showed that our biggest issue was paperwork, what we need to then do is another Pareto on this. For instance, it could be things like dates are missing, signatures are missing, the wrong issue number is on it etc. so again the Pareto will point to the biggest issue within the issue, therefore you know what to fix first." They suddenly realised what Trevor was getting at, they needed to do a deep dive on the top issue to understand what really needed fixing rather than trying to do a general fix. Now that it had been pointed out to them it made sense, and this is the approach that they should have to each of the issues that they come across. Trevor went on "The same is true of when you use the Pareto to show where you are making the most opportunities, by deep diving you can see which part of the business is making the most money and why." Dave, Max and Connor could see the potential of applying a Pareto in this way into their business as it could potentially bring them more work in some areas and reduce or take out work in other areas that was not as profitable. Trevor continued to address the team "Metrics are important as we use these to measure our performance, however we need to have the right metrics and understand exactly what we are trying to measure. I would rather that you have three or four meaningful metrics that you understand thoroughly rather than dozens of metrics that are meaningless to you as it will turn into analysis paralysis because you will spend more time measuring than doing." Trevor could see the team nodding in agreement with him. "So, what you are saying is that less is more." Max clarified. "Absolutely, if we look at it from a waste point of view this would come under over processing. This is something that most organisations get stuck on as they tend to try and measure everything and when it comes to end of month reports, managers can spend days putting the report together, which seniors then ask for a summary of, so they do not always read or understand the metrics, they just collect them because that is what is expected, the important figures that are required by the shareholders are analysed but the rest is just show. This is why you must pick the appropriate metrics for your business." Max was impressed with Trevor's assessment and knowledge and he could now understand why Brian held him in high esteem. "Are there any questions?" Trevor asked. Trevor looked around, but no one had anything to say for the moment. "Thank you for your time, I will let you get back to the build." Trevor dismissed the team.

Dave led the team back to the build, whilst Trevor went over the plans with Max and Connor to understand what the finished build would look like. Amanda decided to make them all a drink as Brian and Nick listened to Max and Connor as they explained the build to Trevor. Just as Amanda, finished making them drinks, Dave appeared and seeing Amanda putting mugs on a tray he went over to her and gave her hand. "What do you think of Trevor?" Dave asked. Amanda explained to Dave how Trevor had come over when she had hit a low point and made her look at her business in a different way that was very positive and gave her the confidence to continue in business. Dave listened carefully, and it confirmed his first impression of Trevor as being a focused individual with a vast amount of experience who was also a very approachable coach and mentor. 'So, what do you think of him?" Amanda asked. "I like him, he is straight talking, and he has a way of making you think." Dave picked up the tray and they joined the others in the office.

Trevor had finished going over the plans as Dave and Amanda appeared with the drinks, which they passed around. They sat and started sipping their teas and coffees and before anyone could start chatting, Trevor asked a question. "How do you think the build is going?" "I think it is going very well" Nick answered. "I agree with Nick" Connor added. Dave decided that he would wait and see what Trevor had to say as he had a feeling there was a lesson coming. Max and Amanda nodded in agreement with Nick and Connor. "What makes you say that?" Trevor asked. "Things are running smoothly, and we are ahead on time and on budget" Connor said with a smile. "So, do you know what was supposed to happen each day?" Trevor persisted. "Well I have a good idea" Connor answered. Trevor nodded to himself "That is what I thought you would say." Trevor took a whiteboard pen, went over to the whiteboard, and drew a table on it.

DAILY AFTER-ACTION REPORT
1.   What was supposed to happen?
2.   What actually happened?
3.   What are the differences between what was supposed to happen and what actually happened?
4.   What can be improved?

Once Trevor had finished, he began to explain what he had drawn. "This is an after-action report that you complete on a daily basis. The idea is to understand what is going on in either this project or within your business." This immediately grabbed everyone's attention and they listened carefully to what Trevor had to say. "We begin by completing section one. This section should be straight forward, as you will have planned in theory what you needed to do for the day. In section two, you need to put in what actually happened that day. In section three you need to identify, what the difference is between what was planned and what actually happened. In section four you identify where you can make improvements, so that the theory and action come closer together. By doing this on a daily basis, you will begin to understand your business better and if you have repeat issues then it shows that your solution the first time around was incorrect because you did not fully get to the root cause. Look for trends and note any potential connections among seemingly unconnected things. Any questions or observations?" Trevor asked. Trevor looked around the group as they took in what he had drawn. He noticed that Dave was rubbing his chin, so he knew that in the short time that he had got to know Dave he would have something to say. "Although this looks simple, this will need some thought" Dave observed. "You are correct Dave, this should not be something that you should hurry, I would say that it should take you on average, once you get used to doing this, about fifteen minutes. The trick is to complete section one at the start of the day, and as you get variation from the planned start to write it down. Where you will spend the most time is in sections three and four." "In effect, this document is lessons learnt. This is where we reflect on how the day has gone" observed Brian. Trevor nodded "Yes Brian, it is about reflection" Trevor confirmed. "That is a powerful document as it will make you think and you will have written evidence for each day that you can compare and build up a picture of your business" observed Max. The others agreed with him as they could all see how this would be useful in their business. Amanda was quite thoughtful. "Correct me if I am wrong, but can you use this in your personal life too?" she asked. "That is a good call Amanda; you can use this in your personal life too, as this will help you to develop yourself by looking how you spend your day and the habits that you may have that could potentially stop you from moving forward." Amanda was pleased that she had spotted another potential use for the daily after-action report that could serve her on a personal level.

Trevor spent the rest of his time on the Gemba walk with Brian, Nick and Amanda. They watched Joe and Trevor spotted something and asked the others if they had seen anything that could be improved. The others watched carefully but they could not see anything out of the ordinary that would draw their attention. After watching for twenty minutes, Trevor decided to share what he had seen. "If you watch Joe you will see he takes a couple of steps between his work and his toolbox, which is waste. Think about how he could eliminate that." The others watched and saw that Trevor was right. "He could just move his toolbox closer" Nick noted. "Yes, he could, but that would mean he would have to lift and move his toolbox." "He could put wheels on his toolbox so that he could move it easily and that way it would always be close to him" Brian suggested. "Good, that is exactly what needs to happen. Tell him what has been spotted and let the team come up with the solution." Brian dutifully went and told Joe what was spotted by Trevor. Joe looked down at his toolbox, then picked the heavy toolbox and moved it closer to him. He would tell the rest of the team later to see if they could come up with a suitable solution. Once they had finished the Gemba walk Trevor informed them that he would have to leave as he had a webinar that he had to go to as he was hosting it. He said his goodbyes to the team and left with the promise that he would return to see the finished build.

Chapter Ten

Amanda and Connor worked with Steve to build a full-size mock-up of the kitchen as Trevor had suggested. It was made up from two by one-inch timber and cardboard and had opening doors and draws so that they could see how it would work in the space. They decided that they would try Connor's layout first and so they positioned everything as per his drawing and checked that the doors and draws did not impede anything. When they had completed the task, they stepped back and checked over their handiwork with a critical eye. "What do you think?" asked Connor. "Actually, it does look quite good as it does maximise the space. However, I don't think it flows when you actually use it." Amanda replied. Then she went on to demonstrate what she meant by role-playing working in the kitchen. "Ok, let's try it your way." They repositioned the mock-up to Amanda's instructions and Connor could see what she meant but it also used up more room, which he pointed out to Amanda. After giving it some thought, Amanda reluctantly agreed with him. They stood looking at the mock-up thinking which way would be best, when Steve spoke up. "Excuse me, but what if we were to change the top so that it was more curved then it could be put further back which would give you more room." "Show us what you mean." Amanda instructed. Steve went off to get some tools, quickly returned, and made the changes to the mock-up and then they repositioned it. They stood back to have a look and were pleased with the outcome. "Well done Steve" Connor told him. "You are a star, and tomorrow I will bring you a home baked cake." Amanda told him enthusiastically. Steve grinned from the recognition he had just been given. "Shall we try the ensuite now?" he asked. "Absolutely, lead the way" Amanda said.

Later Amanda and Connor were in the office with the others and they were telling everyone about the mock-up and how they had maximised the space whilst making it flow. Connor was telling them how much of a big help Steve was. Amanda agreed with Connor and hinted that perhaps he should be given a small pay rise as she had observed that Steve was hard working and was always willing to help. Nick agreed with Amanda and Brian told them that he had also observed the same. Max looked at Connor who nodded perceptively. "What do you think Dave; shall we give young Steve a rise?" Max asked. Dave rubbed his chin as everybody waited to see what he would say. "He is just doing his job, and I expect nothing else." He could see that he was about to get some protests but before anyone said anything he raised his hand to stop it. "However, although he is a hard worker he should not be rewarded just for that, but if we bring this build on time and on budget or better then apart from getting a possible bonus we will give him a rise." Max agreed with the compromise as did Brian as he could understand what Dave was saying and agreed fully with him. Amanda was pleased that she could help Steve be recognised and get him a bit more reward as she honestly thought he deserved it.

The days and weeks went on and the build picked up pace and everything came together. The team continued to apply continuous improvement to everything that they did. The build team particularly enjoyed it as they had turned it into a competition. They had three categories, see who could come up with the most ideas, who could save the most money and who could save the most time. When Dave had promised that the winners would receive a bottle of single malt whisky the competition intensified. Dave found that his team were working not only quicker, but they were also a happier team and instead of complaining about issues they were enthusiastic when they found them as they came up with solutions that went from a straight forward fix to creative ways that Dave did not think his team was capable of. He also found that the quality of the work, which had always been good, was even better and he did not have to go around and point things out to them; there was a definite shift in the culture. It was harder for Brian, Nick and Amanda to find things on their Gemba walks too. On a few occasions, when they did find something and went to point it out, they found that the team was already aware of it and the members were already working on the solution. They had regular visits from building control who were also astounded at the pace of work as well as the quality. This build was the best that they had seen in many a long year and it was always a pleasure to visit the site. Amanda invited the environmental officer to visit on several occasions so that he could see that they had the correct materials that would mitigate the risks of fire etc. and to show him that they had hard wired smoke detectors, emergency lighting etc. He praised them for not skimping and cutting costs and hinted that there were some empty homes on his books that they may want to look at. Amanda was thrilled at the suggestion, as this would help them grow their portfolio and help the council with their housing shortage, so in effect, they would be doing a joint venture with them.

As the rooms became ready, Amanda began to think about the bed and furniture and how they would sit in the room. Taking the idea of the mock-up she decided that she needed something simpler. So, instead of a full mock-up she decided to create the footprint of the bed and furniture out of cardboard, which she then placed in the room as she saw fit and then made the necessary adjustments until she was happy with the positioning. When the supplier delivered the bed and furniture, they placed them as per Amanda's cardboard footprints, so everything went quickly and smoothly, and Amanda was very happy with the final results. The teams were now working on the exterior of the house pointing the bricks and painting the outside walls. Max had a contact who was a landscape gardener and he was now preparing the back garden so that anyone sitting in the new conservatory would have a lovely garden to look out on, he even suggested that they also built a barbeque area on the patio that surrounded the conservatory. Nick thought it was a great idea, so he roped in Mike as the resident brick layer to work with the gardener to come up with a design.

A week later, the house was complete, and the team were starting to pack everything away to move offsite. The house looked fresh and the facelift gave it a great kerb appeal. Inside, it smelt of lavender as Amanda had put in air fresheners throughout the building so that it masked the smell of fresh paint. The walls of the rooms were tastefully painted with a one feature wall and some inexpensive but tasteful paintings were hung in strategic positions. Beds were made, and cushions were placed on the beds and a sprig of lavender was placed on the corner of the bed covers. The en-suite were cleaned and polished and gleamed, ready for use. Curtains were hung and framed the windows as the morning light streamed in. The kitchen/ diner was now functional as the whitegoods had now been installed and Amanda had stored the cooking pots and utensils in the cupboards and drawers. She had also set the table and the sun reflected off the polished stainless-steel cutlery. The lounge furniture was comfortable, and the large flat screen television hung on the wall. The high-speed broadband had also been fitted along with a security system and fire alarm. The house now looked like a show home as they were expecting a visit from the surveyor to value it and from the environmental officer who wanted to look around. They arrived at the same time, which put Amanda in a panic, but Nick and Brian calmed her down with Nick suggesting that he takes the surveyor around and Amanda could show the environmental officer around. Therefore, they split up and went with their respective guests. Nick started by showing the surveyor an album that he and Amanda created with before and after photographs of the build along with scaled down copies of the drawings and more importantly, details of comparable houses showing their value. "As you can see, we have done a lot of work to transform the house both inside and out." The surveyor looked through the album looking to see if he could spot anything out of the ordinary that needed further investigation. Once he had finished looking through the album they went off for a tour beginning outside where the surveyor took out some binoculars, began to survey the roof, and then took his time to have a good look around the outside. Nick was feeling nervous, as the surveyor did not say a lot; he just made notes on the paperwork on his clipboard. They continued into the house where every room was examined in great detail. Over an hour later, the surveyor had finished looking around the property. "You have done a nice job, the quality of the work is one of the best I have seen, and you must have had a great builder." "Yes, we have been lucky with the team, they are a great bunch to work with and I would certainly use them again and recommend them. They brought the project one week under time and under budget." The surveyor raised his eyebrows in surprise. "That is very unusual, no wonder you are pleased with the results. Right down to business, I have taken note of your comparable properties and I can say that I disagree with them" Nick couldn't believe what he was hearing and was about to protest but the surveyor continued talking. "I think that this property is worth ten thousand pounds above their value." Nick face changed from a frown into a big grin. "That is great news, thank you very much." "You're welcome; I will confirm it in writing, so you should have it by next week." They shook hands, the surveyor left, and Nick went off to find Amanda and Brian to tell them the good news. He found Amanda still with the environmental officer; they must have missed each other when they were doing a tour of the house Nick thought. "Hi Nick, this is a great property and I can't believe the finish, it is to a really high standard." "Thank you" Nick replied. "I have just been telling Amanda that I have an empty home just around the corner from here if you want to take a look at it as a possible next project." "We would love to take a look at it" Nick replied, and smile broke out on his face; his day was getting better and better, he thought. "Great, if you pop over to the office on Tuesday I will get the keys and we can come over, so you can assess it." He looked at his watch, "I better get going as I have another appointment shortly." "Thank you for dropping by, and we will see you on Tuesday" Nick replied. They all shook hands and the officer left. Brian was sitting in the office and saw both visitors leave, and a few moments later Nick and Amanda appeared and told him the good news. "Fancy another project Brian?" Nick asked. "Sure, but this time it will not be a freebie, so you would have to factor in my fees this time." Nick did not even hesitate "I am quite prepared to pay your fees." Brian smiled, "You don't even know what I charge, so you may change your mind" he joked. "Not a chance" Nick replied. "Hey look guys." Amanda showed them a social media page on her tablet where she had posted some of the before and after photographs of the property. "Look at all of those positive responses, there must be at least a hundred and I only posted these this morning before coming here." Nick and Brian looked, and they read some of the responses and indeed, they were positive with their comments. "I have the local lettings agent coming tomorrow to take a look and give me a room rental price, let's hope that he is as positive too." "Amanda, what do you think the rooms are worth?" Brian asked. Amanda thought about it for a moment, "I think now that we have a high-quality finish they could go for sixty-five pounds a week, which is good for this area" she replied. "Why don't you advertise them on a free advertising website at eighty-five pounds a week and see what sort of response you get as a test." "I think that is a great idea Brian" Nick replied enthusiastically. Amanda went back to her tablet and found the website that she needed to advertise the property on and she wrote a description and uploaded some photographs then put in the rental cost per room before hitting the submit button. "Ok, all done" she announced. Brian and Nick started chatting about Brian's fees when Connor put his head around the door. "Amanda can I have a word with you please." "Sure Connor" she replied and stepped out of the office to go speak to Connor. "How can I help?" she asked. "I know that you and I have had our small differences." Connor said as he thought back to the argument they had over the layout. "But I have observed how you do things and I respect you for it." "Thank you, Connor," Amanda replied, wondering where this conversation was going. "I have some savings and I would like to invest it with you in your property business, as I am looking for another stream of income." Amanda was taken aback as she was not expecting it. She quickly recovered, "Sure Connor, let's set up a meeting next week where we can discuss it" she replied. Connor smiled as they shook hands and he promised to call in a couple of days when they had all settled down to arrange the meeting. Brian and Nick looked up when Amanda re-joined them. "What was that about?" Nick asked. "Connor wants to invest with us" "Really? Wow I wasn't expecting that." "He is going to call in a couple of days to arrange a meeting for next week." "That is great news; it will certainly help us gain traction to expand our portfolio." "That's what comes when you build up relationships" Brian added. Nick nodded in agreement "Trevor said the same thing to Amanda when he was here last." Nick's mobile phone started ringing; Nick looked at the caller I.D. and excused himself as he took the call. "Hi Jeff" he answered. Nick listened as Jeff told him that the potential investor John, that Nick had been trying to get on board for joint ventures had been in touch as he had seen the photographs of the HMO that Amanda had posted on social media and was impressed with what he had seen. Therefore, he wanted to see a proposal and then based on that, he would possibly arrange a meeting to discuss it further. Nick was elated since the taking on this project opportunities just seemed to appear. This was not something that he was used to, as normally, he had to work very hard to try and create them. He told Amanda and Brian about the potential opportunity that has just come to him and explained to Brian that John was an Angel investor who was a big player. As they were talking, Brian glanced out of the window and saw a car pull up. "Talking about a big player here is Trevor" Brian announced.

Trevor got out of his car, approached the house, took a good look, and nodded to himself. Dave who was supervising the clearing up saw him and went over to greet him. "What do you think?" he asked. "I think that at least from the outside you and your team have done a great job" Trevor replied. "I will get Amanda to show you around, as I don't want to mess the place up with my dirty shoes and overalls." Dave quickly went off to get Amanda. A few moments later, she appeared with Dave and after greeting Trevor, she led him to the house and took him for a tour around it. Trevor was pleased with the outcome; the finish was to a high standard of quality and was tastefully decorated. When they had finished looking around the house, they headed back to the office where Trevor greeted the others. "What do you think of it?" Nick asked anxiously. "I think that this is a great property, everything from the architecture to the build standard and the decoration is of high standard and most importantly, it was also brought in under your budget and under time. Therefore, the team have done extremely well, and they have certainly earnt their bonus" Trevor replied. "And I am happy to pay it" Nick replied. Trevor smiled, as he knew that when it came to money Nick tried to save as much as possible, so this was a turnaround for him. "If anything, what have you learnt doing this project?" Trevor asked. Nick and Amanda pointed out all of the new skills that they had learnt, how to understand the costs associated with project and how to save time and money without having to skimp on the project. They spoke for a good twenty minutes of their experiences from their own perspective. "So how would you summarise it in a short sentence?" Trevor asked them. This question was hard, they thought; but also typical of Trevor as he was making them think. Trevor waited as they thought about it. "Attention to detail, strive for good quality and continuous improvement and do not accept the status quo." "Well done Amanda. How about you Nick?" "Pay attention to quality, strive for continuous improvement and the bottom line will take of itself" Nick replied. "Very good Nick. You have both summarised it quite well, but you have both missed out an important element." Nick and Amanda looked puzzled, until Trevor continued. "You have to have a great team around you as you cannot do this sort of project on your own, so teamwork is also key to success." They both knew that Trevor was right, without Dave and his team, Max, Connor and especially Brian this would never have happened. They were also thankful that Trevor decided to help them and started the momentum that allowed this to happen. So, they agreed wholeheartedly with Trevor. "What is next?" Trevor asked. Nick and Amanda told him about the empty homes, one of which they will be visiting next week, also about Connor wanting to invest with them and about the Angel investor John. "Things are looking up for you, just keep the momentum going. Have you thought about what sort of proposal you want to send to your Angel investor?" Trevor asked. Nick smiled "I have a forty-page document that tells an investor all about our area, what we invest in and all about the company." Nick replied with a touch of pride. Trevor frowned "At this stage, I don't think that is the right approach." "Why, it's a great document?" asked Nick starting to sound a little bit defensive. "When you are dealing with investors they just want to keep things quick and simple, they don't want to have to read pages and pages at an early stage. This comes under one of the wastes, over processing. What you need is a simple one-page document, if they want to know more about you and your company they will ask you and that is when you can give them your main company document." Nick was thinking about all of the information that was in the document and could not see how he could just pick out relevant information, as it was all relevant as far as he was concerned. "But how do I fit a proposal onto one page?" Nick asked. "Can I use your laptop please Brian?" Brian took out his laptop and powered it up so that Trevor could use it. Trevor quickly produced a table then he searched the internet for a picture of a house, which he added to the table, then he started to populate the table and within ten minutes produced an example of a one-page document proposal. "There, that should suffice. You see, your investor will only be initially interested in one deal, and if he is happy with it then he will go ahead with it. If he is happy with the outcome, then there will be more deals." This made sense and Nick and Amanda could see that the one page had all the information that an investor would be interested in, so it was a powerful document.

NAC Properties, Solihull	
Proposal	**Plan**
8% ROI	6 Bedroom HMO for Professionals
Current Deal	**Exit Strategy**
 Grade 2 listed Detached 6-bedroom House in Solihull	Preferred strategy is 6 Bedroom HMO It can also work as a Serviced Accommodation The property is also feasible as a family Buy to Let It can also be refurbished and sold as a Flip
Analysis	**Return on Investment**
Purchase Price £150,000 Stamp Duty £12,000 Legal Fees £2,000 Refurbishment £10,000 Deposit £37,500 Done Up Value £200,000 Rental as HMO £2,080 per Month Rental per Annum £24,960 Monthly Cash Flow £997.50 **Note:** All our figures are conservative estimates based on a worst-case scenario and we have stress tested them at a 6% mortgage rate. A number of letting agents have confirmed the rental demand for this type of property in this area.	We are looking to raise £70,000 to cover the buying and refurbishment with some contingency cost The term will be for a maximum of 9 Months, for which we are offering 8% per annum **Note:** We have confirmed the 'done up value' at between £200,000 & £250,000, via three estate agents and market information and we intend to re-mortgage the property after 6 months ownership to release the equity and repay the sum borrowed.
Further information about our company, our experience and the area are available upon request.	

Nick studied the document and could see that it was an elegant but simple solution to propose a deal that gave the facts without going into great detail. In fact, he thought if he was presented with something like this he could make up his mind in minutes of whether he wanted to invest or not and based on the information in the example he would. "That is a great document; could I have a copy as a template?" Nick asked. "Sure Nick, have you got a memory stick or would you like Brian to email it to you?" Nick reached into his pocket and pulled out a small stainless-steel memory stick. "There you go." Nick handed the memory stick to Trevor who then attached it to Brian's laptop and uploaded the document to it. Trevor looked at his watch, "I'm sorry but I will have to go as I have another appointment, but we will stay in touch. Brian, I will see you next week." They shook hands with Trevor and said their goodbyes to him. Trevor then went and found Dave and said goodbye to him and his team before getting into his car to drive off for his next appointment.

A week later, Nick was sitting at home feeling very pleased that the house now had full occupancy with each tenant happily paying ninety pounds a week for their double bed rooms. They had visited one of the empty homes with Dave and Connor, which they had decided to take on much to the delight of the environmental officer, and the investor liked Nick's one-page proposal, so he had a meeting set up for the following week. Nick's contact in Spain had rang him about a property on the Granada coast that he was flying out to visit with Amanda that afternoon. Whilst Nick was reflecting, Amanda was interviewing for their first employee and she felt happy, as this was a good sign that the business was growing.

A few days later, they returned from Spain and were happy with the purchase of the property that they had gone to view. Although the paperwork will still need to be completed to obtain the deeds, they did have a set of keys for it. Nick tasked Amanda with packaging the keys up with the address and a thank you note for Trevor, whilst he made a journey that he had been putting off for a long time.

Nick parked his car in the road outside a well-kept and tidy council house. He got out of his car and taking a deep breath, he went up to the small gate, opened it and walked through. Closing the gate behind him, he walked up to the front door. Taking another deep breath, he raised his hand and pressed the doorbell. He waited a few moments and the door opened, and before him stood his father. Before Nick could clear his throat to speak, his father spoke first. "Hello son, it's been a long time." His father then turned his head towards the hall and shouted. "Ma, put the kettle on, our Nick is here." He then turned towards Nick, "You better come in son; we have some catching up to do." He stood aside to let Nick in. Nick tried to hold back the tears that he felt welling up and stepped into his childhood home. A moment later Nick's mother appeared, she took one look and rushed up to him and threw her arms around his neck and hugged him. Nick could not hold back his tears any longer; he hugged her back, and the feeling of warmth and love rushing to him like an express train. After a few minutes, they broke apart and his mother led him through to the heart of the home, her kitchen where he sat down at the table whilst his mother made a fuss of him. His dad sat opposite him and smiled at the site of Nick and his mother's reaction. They finally all sat down together with drinks in front of each of them, then his dad asked, "Well son, tell us what you have been doing all of these years?" Nick took a deep breath trying to decide where to start "Well dad."

Useful Books and websites

Quality & Continuous Improvement

Out of the Crisis by W. Edwards Deming, 2000 MIT Press

Juran's Quality Handbook: The Complete Guide to Performance Excellence by J M Juran & J A Defeo, June 2010 McGraw-Hill Education

The Toyota Way: 14 Management Principles from the World's Greatest Manufacturer by Jeffrey Liker, 2004 McGraw-Hill Professional

The Goal: A Process of Ongoing Improvement by Eliyahu M. Goldratt & Jeff Cox, 2004 Gower

Lean Acres: A Tale of Strategic Innovation and Improvement in a Farm-iliar Setting by Jim Bowie, 2011 American Society for Quality

BS EN ISO 9001:2015 by CEN, 2015 CEN-CENELEC Management Centre

Learning to See by Mike Rother and John Shook, October 2009, Lean Enterprise Institute, Inc.

Scrum: The art of doing twice the work in half the time by Jeff Sutherland, August 2015 Random House

Toyota Kata: Managing People for Improvement, Adaptiveness and Superior Results by Mike Rother, McGraw-Hill Education; 1st edition Sept. 2009

Critical Chain Management by Goldratt, Eliyahu M, September 1997 North River Press

Deming's Profound Changes: When Will the Sleeping Giant Awaken? by Kenneth T Delavigne, Pearson Technology Group; Facsimile edition Jan. 2008

Dr Deming: The American Who Taught the Japanese About Quality by Rafael Aguayo, Touchstone; 1st Fireside Ed edition Sept. 1991

Our Iceberg is Melting: Changing and Succeeding Under Any Conditions by John Kotter & Holger Rathgeber, Macmillan; Reprints edition Sept. 2006

That's Not How We Do It Here! A Story About How Organizations Rise, Fall - and Can Rise Again by John Kotter & Holger Rathgeber, Portfolio Penguin Jun. 2016

Self-Help

Step Up and F.O.C.U.S: by Lindsay Hopkins, 2014 Create Space Independent Publishing Platform

4@13@7 System: by Lindsay Hopkins, 2014 CreateSpace Independent Publishing Platform

The Slight Edge by Jeff Olson, October 2013 Gazelle

The One Thing by Gary Keller and Jay Papasan, April 2014, John Murray Learning

The Richest Man in Babylon by George Samuel Clason, February 2004, Signet

Think and Grow Rich by Napoleon Hill, September 2007, Wilder Publications

See You at the Top (Motivational series) by Zig Zaglar, Pelican Publishing Co; Revised edition Dec. 1975

Feel The Fear and Do It Anyway: How to Turn Your Fear and Indecision into Confidence and Action by Susan Jeffers, Vermilion; Revised edition 4 Jan. 2007

Websites

American Society for Quality http://asq.org/index.aspx

Architects Registration Board http://www.arb.org.uk/

Building contracts, building tips www.diydoctor.org.uk

Building Costs http://www.quotationcheck.com/

Charted Quality Institute www.thecqi.org

Critical Chain http://www.dbrmfg.co.nz/Projects%20Critical%20 Chain.htm

HSE – CDM 2015 http://www.hse.gov.uk/pubns/books/l153.htm

Landlords National Property Group https://www.lnpg.co.uk/

Lean in Construction http://leanconstruction.org.uk/

Lean UK http://www.leanuk.org/

Lean US http://www.lean.org/

Quality Digest http://www.qualitydigest.com/

The Royal Institute of British Architects https://www.architecture.com/Explore/Home.aspx

Legal Documents http://www.rocketlawyer.co.uk

Windsor & Patania Architects http://windsorpatania.com/

About the author

John Foster is a Chartered Quality Professional with a sharp sense of what it takes to drive results effectively. He has years of high-level experience in engineering and has specialised in lean and total quality management. John has worked with many entrepreneurs to help them maximise their profits and time and has become known for his ability to provide sound advice with regards to property investment, Amazon FBA, and a range of other businesses. Valued for his far-reaching expertise as much as for his unbeatable work ethics, he is a highly sought-after consultant and coach. He knows how to manage projects as well as people and is used to perform under pressure, whilst still delivering the desired results.

As a speaker, John is approachable and captivating. His knack for coaching and leading others are reflected when he addresses an audience. John strongly believes in the concept of ongoing education, seeking constantly to expand his base of knowledge to better serve his clients.

John is currently leading a team and using his expertise in problem solving and human factors to provide a quick and practical problem-solving method that can be used in the UK healthcare system

John lives in Solihull with his partner Georgina. Besides property, quality and continuous improvement, his hobbies and interests include Motorsports, Photography, History, Travelling and Reading. John is also fluent in Spanish and is known amongst family and friends for his ability to make great Sangria. John's motto is 'No matter what you do or where you go always add value'

12625876R00140

Printed in Great Britain
by Amazon